Poultry Dishes

DAVID & CHARLES

Newton Abbot London

British Library Cataloguing in Publication Data
Poultry dishes.—(David & Charles Kitchen Workshop)
   1. Cookery (Poultry)
   I. Fjaerkre. *English*
   641.6'65   TX750

ISBN 0-7153-8462-7

Filmset by MS Filmsetting Limited, Frome, Somerset
and printed in The Netherlands
by Smeets Offset BV, Weert
for David & Charles (Publishers) Limited
Brunel House, Newton Abbot, Devon

Poultry

Farm-reared poultry of all kinds, including poussins, chickens, boiling fowls, ducks, geese and turkeys are the subjects of this book. As well as featuring interesting and often unusual recipes, it also contains helpful information on how to deal with fresh and frozen poultry, how to joint and carve it, and how to cook and flavour it to best effect.

The dishes include both quick and easy recipes, some of them using ready cooked chicken, and more exotic party fare which, although it takes a little longer to prepare, is well worth the effort.

Buying Poultry

All the different types of poultry described on the following pages are available frozen nearly all the year round, with the possible exception of geese. Birds are bred to provide plump poultry with a high proportion of breast meat. Fresh chickens are always on sale, but fresh ducks, geese and turkeys may only be in the shops at certain seasons of the year. Most poultry is sold oven ready, that is, plucked and drawn (gutted), which makes them simple to prepare for cooking. The giblets – liver, heart and gizzard – are usually wrapped and tucked inside the bird before it is sold.

The quality of frozen poultry is carefully controlled, and is only very rarely a cause for concern, but you should check that the wrapping is intact, and that there are no signs of dark markings on the skin. Always remember to check the sell-by date on the label if there is one.

When buying fresh poultry, it is essential to make sure that the bird is young and tender. The best way to do this is to examine the beak, which in young birds is pale in colour and easily bent at the bridge. Legs and feet should be covered in supple skin, and the claws should be pointed.

If plucked, the bird should have a pale, unblemished skin with no scars or dark spots or patches. The pale skin of ducks and geese is marked with a characteristic checked pattern. The fat should not be excessive in quantity and should be pale or clear yellow in colour and evenly distributed over the body of the bird.

When cleaned and prepared for cooking, an unplucked bird will lose 20 to 30 per cent of its weight, so it is important to calculate this – and make due allowance for it – when buying poultry.

Chickens

Chicken, with its fine-textured, mildly flavoured, lean and easily digested meat is popular with adults and children alike. It is available all the year round, both fresh and frozen, and is ideal for a huge variety of dishes. The great majority of chicken is now bought frozen, and the meat keeps its quality well even after long periods at below zero temperatures. To retain the succulence of the flesh it is best to defrost chickens and most other poultry slowly – preferably in the refrigerator – which takes at least 24 hours. It can also be defrosted at room temperature and this will take 10–12 hours for an average-sized bird.

Chickens are given different names according to their size, the quality of their meat and the way they are reared. The smallest, most tender chickens are described as poussins and weigh $\frac{1}{2}$–1kg (1–2lb). A spring chicken or double poussin weighs around $1\frac{1}{4}$kg ($2\frac{1}{2}$lb). Ordinary fresh and frozen chickens, usually labelled as roasting or oven ready birds, come in the middle range of weights, and are reared to provide the maximum possible amount of meat for your money. They weigh up to 2kg ($4\frac{1}{2}$lb) or even a little more.

The largest chickens on the market are plump capons, which are emasculated male birds specially reared for the table. They weigh up to 5kg (11lb). Boiling fowls are birds usually on the heavy side but compared with ordinary chickens are older and are not suitable for roasting or grilling. When boiled or poached, however, their meat is succulent and full of flavour.

In recipes involving boiling or poaching, any kind of chicken of the correct weight may be used. It is not necessary to use a boiling fowl.

Chicken giblets are rich in vitamins and minerals. Finely chopped they can be added to stuffings and sauces, or used on their own for pâtés, soups and other nourishing meals.

Turkey

Good quality turkey meat is finely textured, pale and lean. Roast turkey makes excellent party fare for a crowd, but there are many other ways in which turkey can be prepared. Except at Christmas, turkeys are only widely available in their frozen form, but are also sold as frozen portions and half or quarter birds. Unless the wrapper states otherwise, the giblets should be included, and will be found inside the body or neck cavity of the bird.

A turkey weighs from about 2.5 to 10kg ($5\frac{1}{2}$ to 25lb). A bird at the lowest end of the weight range will serve 4 people, while a bird weighing 4–5kg (9–$12\frac{1}{2}$lb) will provide ample meat for 8–10 guests.

Frozen turkey is best defrosted at room temperature, and this will take a minimum of 12 hours for the smallest bird. Defrosting in the refrigerator takes about double the time.

Turkeys can be stuffed with traditional chestnut and sausagemeat or sage, onion and breadcrumb stuffing. Fruit, minced meat and a variety of vegetables also complement the flavour of the meat well. Any left-over turkey is ideal for salads, casseroles and for setting in aspic.

Duck and Goose

Ducks and geese are fatty birds particularly suitable for roasting, since this method of cooking draws out the fat from the flesh. Apples, prunes and oranges are fruits which go well with these birds because they take the edge off the richness of the meat. Like turkeys, ducks are most widely available frozen, but geese are usually sold fresh for a limited season around the Christmas period.

An average duck weighs from about 1.3kg to 2.5kg ($2\frac{3}{4}$ to $5\frac{1}{2}$lb) and serves 3 to 6 people. A goose weighs from about 3 to 6kg ($6\frac{3}{4}$ to $13\frac{1}{2}$lb) and will serve 5–10. As well as traditional roasting, ducks and geese may be fried, salted and boiled with excellent results. The meat is good cold, and duck salad is certainly to be recommended.

Adding Flavour to Poultry Marinating

Marinating any poultry vastly improves the flavour of the meat and makes it more tender and succulent. A good all purpose marinade should contain oil and red or white wine or a good quality wine vinegar, plus seasonings, spices and herbs of your choice. For preference, use olive oil, and choose a vinegar flavoured with tarragon.

The following herbs and spices complement any poultry:

Parsley, chives, tarragon, rosemary, thyme, basil, marjoram, bay leaves and sage.

Juniper berries, nutmeg, cinnamon, cardamom, coriander, ginger, caraway, paprika, cayenne, saffron, cloves, black and white pepper, allspice and curry powder or garam masala.

In place of red or white wine, try adding sherry, port or Madeira to a marinade – or add a dash of soy sauce or mushroom ketchup.

Other flavourings worth experimenting with are chopped onion, crushed garlic and finely grated or thinly pared lemon or orange zest.

Dry Spicing

Poultry that is going to be fried or roasted and has not been marinated should be rubbed with oil and/or softened butter and sprinkled with herbs and spices of your choice before cooking to improve the flavour of the meat.

Bouquet Garni

When boiling or casseroling a chicken you can add herbs and spices to the water, but more usually a bouquet garni is made. This consists of bay leaves, parsley sprigs and a few celery leaves, plus sprigs of other herbs. These may be tied together or wrapped in muslin. When the bouquet garni is completely wrapped, dried herbs may be used and you can add peppercorns, whole cloves or strips of orange or lemon zest.

The Versatile Chicken

Chicken can be cooked in a vast number of different ways and served for main meals or snacks at any time.
The recipes here and overleaf show how you can serve chicken as a starter, as a family supper or make it special enough to be dinner party fare.

Mandarin Chicken
(serves 4)
Preparation time: about 15 min plus roasting
Unsuitable for the freezer

1 roast or pot roasted chicken
1 crisp lettuce or Chinese cabbage
25–40g (1–1½oz) butter
salt, pepper
300–400ml (½–¾pt) natural yoghurt
1 small can mandarin oranges

1 While the chicken is still hot, cut it into 4 portions and place on an ovenproof dish. Keep warm in the oven or a warming drawer.
2 Trim the lettuce, chop it coarsely, then sauté in butter for a couple of minutes until heated through, but not soft. Season with salt and pepper. Heat the yoghurt through carefully, but do not allow it to separate.
3 Arrange the lettuce around the chicken pieces. Pour yoghurt over and garnish with mandarin segments.
Serve at once with boiled rice or French bread.

Top, left to right: Chicken Drumsticks with Vegetables (page 9), Marinated Chicken (page 8), Pot Roast Chicken (page 12), Chicken Ragoût with Giblets (page 8) and a Chicken Salad (pages 38–39).
Bottom, left to right: Chicken Liver Pâté (page 8), Mandarin Chicken (above) and Chicken Pilaff (page 8).

Chicken Liver Pâté

(serves 4–5)
Preparation time: about 30 min
Cooling time: at least 2 hr
Suitable for the freezer

about 350g (¾lb) frozen chicken
  livers
about 100g (¼lb) butter
salt, black pepper
1 small portion of boiled or fried
  chicken, skinned and boned
4 × 15ml tbsp (4–5tbsp) dry sherry
or 2 × 15ml tbsp (2tbsp) brandy
marjoram
thyme

1 Defrost and trim livers. Dry well, then fry for 2 min on both sides in 15–25g (½–1oz) butter. Season with a pinch of salt and pepper and leave to cool for a while.
2 Pass the liver through a sieve and mix with finely chopped chicken meat and remaining, softened butter. Alternatively, work the livers, chicken meat and butter in a blender to form a smooth purée.
3 Add the sherry or brandy, then season with a pinch of thyme and marjoram and salt and pepper to taste. Pour into a small dish, cover with foil and refrigerate until firm. Turn out on to a serving dish and garnish with sliced raw mushrooms, sprinkled with in lemon juice to prevent them from discolouring.
Serve as a first course or as a light lunch dish accompanied by toast and watercress.

Chicken Ragoût with Giblets

(serves 4)
Preparation time: about 15 min
Cooking time: 1–1¼ hr
Suitable for the freezer

1 small cooked chicken
heart and gizzard from chicken
4 rashers bacon
2 onions
25g (1oz) butter
1 can tomatoes
1 × 5ml tsp (1tsp) dried basil
thyme, marjoram
salt, pepper
lemon juice

1 Skin and bone the chicken and cut the meat into bite-sized pieces. Cut the heart and gizzard into small strips.
2 Remove the rinds from the bacon and chop into small pieces. Peel and chop the onion. Fry the bacon, onion, heart and gizzard in the butter in a flameproof casserole until golden brown. Sprinkle with salt and pepper and add tomatoes, including all the juice. Simmer for about 30 min.
3 Season with basil, a pinch of dried thyme and marjoram and lemon juice then simmer for further 30 min. Taste and season with more salt if necessary, then add the chicken slices and warm through over low heat.
Serve straight from the casserole with fluffy mashed potatoes and a simple salad.

Chicken Pilaff

(serves 4)
Preparation time: about 30 min
Marinating time: ½–1 hr
Cooking time: about 30 min
Suitable for the freezer, but will lose a little of its flavour

4 chicken joints
salt
butter
For the marinade:
2 × 15ml tbsp (2tbsp) oil
juice of 1 lemon
½ × 5ml tsp (½tsp) pepper
1 crushed garlic clove
1 × 15ml tbsp (1tbsp) soy sauce
For the pilaff:
1 large onion
40g (1½oz) butter
1 × 15ml tbsp (1tbsp) oil
175g (6oz) long-grain rice
450ml (17fl oz) stock
salt, pepper
paprika
50g (2oz) sultanas
50g (2oz) walnuts

1 Dry the chicken joints well and place in a shallow dish. Mix together the lemon juice, oil, pepper, garlic and soy sauce and pour over meat. Leave to marinate in the refrigerator for ½–1 hr.
2 Peel and finely chop the onion and sauté carefully in a heavy-based saucepan in 15g (½oz) butter and 1 × 15ml tbsp (1tbsp) oil until soft and translucent but not brown. Add the rice and cook, stirring until it is white and has lost its transparency. Add the hot stock, ½–1 × 5ml tsp (½–1tsp) salt, a large pinch of pepper and ½ × 5ml tsp (½tsp) paprika. Stir to mix well then cover with a tightly fitting lid. Simmer for about 20 min.
3 Meanwhile remove chicken joints from marinade and dry well. Fry chicken in 25g (1oz) butter over medium heat, turning frequently. Sprinkle with salt and keep warm.
4 Chop walnuts coarsely and sauté carefully in the remaining butter. Add the sultanas and the marinade and stir into the cooked rice. Put the rice in a very low oven or over the lowest possible heat, forking through carefully from time to time. Arrange the chicken and rice in a warmed serving dish and serve immediately with a green salad. Mango chutney goes well with this dish.

Marinated Chicken

(serves 4–6)
Preparation time: about 20 min
Defrosting time: 10–12 hr
Marinating time: 1–2 hr
Cooking time: 30–40 min
Suitable for the freezer without egg yolks added

1 large frozen oven-ready chicken
salt, 2 egg yolks
100ml (4fl oz) double cream
finely chopped parsley
For the marinade:
juice of 1 lemon and 1 orange
1 garlic clove
4 whole cloves
½ × 5ml tsp (½tsp) dried oregano

1 Defrost the chicken slowly in the refrigerator. Cut into 6 or 8 portions.
2 Make the marinade: mix together the lemon and orange juice, then add crushed garlic, cloves and oregano. Place the chicken in a shallow dish and sprinkle with marinade. Set aside in a cold place for 1–2 hr.
3 Transfer the meat and marinade to a large saucepan. Remove cloves and add 1 × 5ml tsp (1tsp) salt and enough water to barely cover the chicken. Simmer, partially covered, until the meat is tender.
4 Remove the pan from the heat, take out the chicken portions and transfer to a hot dish. Whisk the egg yolks with the cream and stir into the stock. Return the pan to the stove and heat until nearly boiling. Season with salt, pour over the chicken and sprinkle with finely chopped parsley.
Serve hot with boiled potatoes or French bread and a green salad.

Chicken Drumsticks with Vegetables

(serves 4)
Preparation time: about 15 min
Marinating time: 3–4 hr
Cooking time: 35–45 min
Unsuitable for the freezer

6–8 chicken drumsticks
40g (1½oz) butter
1 × 15ml tbsp (1tbsp) oil
2 large onions
1 × 5ml tsp (1tsp) paprika
250g (9oz) mushrooms
½–1 lettuce
salt, pepper
For the marinade :
4 × 15ml tbsp (4tbsp) oil
3 × 15ml tbsp (3tbsp) lemon juice
1–2 × 15ml tbsp (1–2tbsp) soy sauce
1 crushed garlic clove
½ × 5ml tsp (½tsp) pepper
½ × 5ml tsp (½tsp) crushed rosemary

1 Arrange the chicken drumsticks in a shallow dish. Mix together all the marinade ingredients, pour over the chicken and leave for 3–4 hr.
2 Dry meat lightly with kitchen paper then sauté in 25g (1oz) butter over moderate heat. When the chicken is well browned on all sides, season with salt and pour over the marinade.
3 Clean, prepare and chop all the vegetables. Sauté the onion in the remaining butter and oil. Add the other vegetables and stir fry over little heat for a few minutes. The vegetables should be tender but still crisp. Season the vegetables to taste with salt and pepper and arrange on a dish. Arrange the drumsticks on top and finally pour over the cooking juices from the chicken. Serve at once with wholemeal bread and a tossed green salad or a tomato salad.

Bean and Chicken Casserole

(serves 4)
Preparation time: about 20 min
Cooking time: 45–50 min
Oven temperature: 190°C, 375°F, Gas 5
Unsuitable for the freezer

1 oven-ready chicken
1 × 15ml tbsp (1tbsp) oil
2 onions
15g (½oz) butter
⅛–¼ × 5ml tsp (⅛–¼tsp) chilli powder
1 × 15ml tbsp (1tbsp) plain flour
200ml chicken stock (made with a cube)
1 small can tomatoes
1 can baked beans in tomato sauce
salt, black pepper

1 Cut the chicken into 6–8 portions and fry in oil until golden.
2 Peel onion and slice into thin rings. Sauté onion rings in butter in an ovenproof casserole, add chilli powder and flour and simmer for a couple of minutes. Pour in the stock and add the tomatoes, including all the juice. Bring to the boil and add the chicken.
3 Cover with a lid or foil and bake in a pre-heated oven. Ten minutes before the end of cooking time, mix in the beans, taste and season.
Serve piping hot with French bread and a green salad.

Below : Deep-fried Chicken Pieces (see page 25).

9

Roast Chicken

Chickens can be roasted in several different ways. You can open roast them in an ovenproof dish or roasting tin, cook them in a film roasting bag or use a terracotta chicken brick.

Chicken in a Brick

Immerse both halves of the chicken brick in cold water for 24 hours if you are using the brick for the first time. Otherwise, soak it for about 30 min. Season the chicken inside and out, put some parsley sprigs inside it and place in the brick. Surround the chicken with a mixture of dried fruit soaked in water for about 2 hr and/or with a mixture of sliced vegetables such as onions, carrots, leeks and celery.

Put on the lid and cook in the oven at a temperature of 230–250°C, 450–475°F, Gas 8–9 for 1–1½ hr. The clay of which the brick is made distributes the heat evenly and makes the chicken crisp and brown all over. For an extra crisp finish, remove the lid for the last 10–15 min of cooking. The juices that collect in the brick are so concentrated that you can dilute them with a little stock or water to make the gravy. Or they can be used as the basis of a tasty cream or soured cream sauce.

As well as the fruit and vegetables from the brick, you can serve potato croquettes or jacket potatoes.

Open Roast Chicken

Season the inside of a well dried oven-ready chicken with salt and pepper. Put a few sprigs of parsley and a knob of butter inside, then season the inside with salt and pepper and smooth on some softened butter.

Place the chicken breast uppermost in an ovenproof dish or small roasting tin and pour in enough stock to barely cover the base of the dish or tin. Roast for 1–1¼ hr at 230°C, 450°F, Gas 8, replenishing the stock as necessary. Serve with bread sauce and a green salad.

Roasting Bag

See recipe for Stuffed Chicken on the next page.

Stuffed Chicken

(serves 5–6)
Preparation time: about 30 min
Cooking time: about 1½ hr
Oven temperature (bottom shelf):
200°C, 400°F, Gas 6
Unsuitable for the freezer

*1 chicken weighing 1.1–1.3kg
    (2½–3lb)*
salt, pepper
butter
For the stuffing :
*about 300g (11oz) minced pork
    or minced pork and veal*
1 × 5ml tsp (1tsp) salt
½ × 5ml tsp (½tsp) pepper
1 × 15ml tbsp (1tbsp) breadcrumbs
1 egg white
75–100ml (3–4fl oz) light stock
about 75ml (3fl oz) double cream
6–7 crushed juniper berries
*4 × 15ml tbsp (4tbsp) dry port or
    Madeira*
For the sauce :
meat juices
100–200ml (4–7fl oz) double cream
salt, pepper
port or Madeira

Above : Stuffed Chicken in a roasting bag. Below : Chicken in a Brick.

1 Wipe the chicken inside and out with a damp cloth. Mix together all the stuffing ingredients and set aside for about ½ hr. Stir the stuffing and add more cream if necessary.

2 Season the inside of the chicken with salt and pepper, then season the outside with salt. Fill with ¾ of the mince and close opening with skewers. Place the remaining stuffing in a greased, ovenproof dish.

3 Season the outside of the chicken with 25–40g (1–1½oz) softened butter and place in a roasting bag big enough to hold it comfortably. Close with clips and make several holes in the base. Place the chicken breast uppermost in an ovenproof dish or tin and roast for about 1½ hr. Put the reserved stuffing in the oven for the last 25 min of cooking time.

4 Open the cooking bag and allow all the gravy to run out. Strain into a saucepan and add any juices from the separately cooked stuffing. Turn off the oven then return the chicken to it, uncovered.

5 Add the cream to the gravy and bring to the boil. Season with salt and pepper and port or Madeira. Slice the stuffing and serve with the chicken and sauce. French bread and a green salad go well with this.

11

2 In a flameproof casserole, brown both chickens on all sides in 15g (½oz) butter over moderate heat. Turn chickens by using 2 wooden spoons to prevent the skin splitting. Season with salt.

3 Lower the heat, add the remaining butter to the casserole and turn the chickens on their sides. Put on the lid and simmer until tender, turning from time to time.

4 Dish up the chickens and keep warm. Add the stock and deglaze the pan. Season to taste. Cut each chicken in half lengthways. Serve the sauce, potato croquettes and steamed vegetables.

Pot roast a large chicken, weighing about 1.1kg (2½lb) in the same way, but lengthen the cooking time. To serve cut into quarters.

VARIATION
Old-fashioned Roast Chicken in Cream Sauce

Fill 2 poussins or 1 oven-ready chicken with plenty of washed sprigs of parsley and about 50g (2oz) butter. Roast as indicated in previous recipe, but without stock.

After the chicken has been browned sprinkle with a little cream, simmering on low heat.

When the chicken is cooked, keep warm and deglaze the casserole with 300–400ml (½–¾pt) double cream. Boil, then add a couple of drops of vinegar – the cream sauce will curdle, and this is intentional. Season with salt and pepper.

Cut the chickens into serving portions, trim and serve with the cream sauce, plus parsley-sprinkled potatoes and a cucumber salad.

Pot Roast Chicken

Whether you roast your chicken whole or in portions, tasty results are guaranteed. The tender vegetables and the scrumptious sauces make this filling but delicious. The only accompaniment it needs is rice, potatoes or simply a fresh, crusty French loaf.

Pot Roast Chicken
(serves 4)
Preparation time: 10–15 min
Cooking time: about 45 min
Suitable for the freezer, but loses a little of its flavour

2 poussins or spring chickens, each weighing about 700g (1½lb)
salt, pepper
parsley
75–100g (3–4oz) butter
200–300ml (7–10fl oz) stock

1 Wipe the chickens with a damp cloth. Season the inside with salt and pepper and place several parsley sprigs and 15g (½oz) butter inside each.

Curried Spicy Chicken
(serves 4–6)
Preparation time: about 20 min
Cooking time: 35–45 min
Suitable for the freezer

2 spring chickens, each weighing 700–800g (1½–2lb)
2 onions
1 garlic clove
15–25g (½–1oz) butter
1–2 × 15ml tbsp (1–2tbsp) oil
curry powder
salt, pepper
100ml (4fl oz) natural yoghurt
1 cooking apple
4 ripe tomatoes
½ × 5ml tsp (½tsp) ginger

Rice stuffing, flavoured with onion, garlic, spices and herbs, adds a Mediterranean flavour to Spanish Pot Roast.

$\frac{1}{2} \times 5ml$ tsp ($\frac{1}{2}$tsp) coriander
300–400ml ($\frac{1}{2}$–$\frac{3}{4}$pt) stock
150–200ml (5–7fl oz) thick soured cream

1 Cut each chicken into 4. Dry well. Brown chicken pieces on all sides in a mixture of butter and oil in wide casserole. Add chopped onions, crushed garlic and 3–4 × 5ml tsp (3–4tsp) curry powder. Simmer for about 5 min over low heat, turning the chicken pieces from time to time. Sprinkle with a little salt and pepper.

2 Pour yoghurt into casserole. Simmer for further 5 min until the yoghurt is very thick, again turning the chicken from time to time. Wash the apple and grate straight into casserole. Peel and quarter tomatoes. Add to the casserole with ginger and coriander and a little salt and pepper. Pour over the stock and simmer until the chicken is tender.

3. Meanwhile, boil enough rice to serve your guests (follow the weight given on the packet) in chicken stock. Remove the chicken pieces from the casserole and keep warm. Stir the soured cream into meat juices and boil for a while uncovered. Season with salt and pepper and pour sauce over chicken. Serve with rice and garnish with mango chutney, thin strips of raw red or green pepper and curried bananas: peel small, even sized bananas and fry until golden in oil, then add a little curry powder (do not fry for too long, or they will turn mushy). Sprinkle the cooked bananas with lemon juice and serve warm.

Spanish Pot Roast

(serves 4)
Preparation time: about 20 min
Cooking time: 50–60 min
Unsuitable for the freezer

1 large oven-ready chicken
salt, pepper
butter, oil
200ml (7fl oz) stock
For the stuffing:
1 onion

1 garlic clove
1 × 15ml tbsp (1tbsp) oil
75g (3oz) long-grain rice
200ml (7fl oz) chicken stock
6 × 15ml tbsp (6tbsp) finely chopped parsley
tarragon, chervil or other green herbs
2 small eggs
salt, pepper

1 Chop the onion and crush the garlic for the stuffing. Turn together in oil on low heat and stir in the rice. Allow to colour slightly, add the warmed stock and boil, covered, for 18 min over low heat.

2 Fluff up the cooked rice with a fork and add the lightly beaten eggs, parsley and other herbs to taste.

3 Wipe the prepared broiler with a damp cloth and rub with salt and pepper. Add the rice stuffing and close opening with metal skewers (see small illustrations on page 14).

4 Fry the chicken in equal quantities of butter and oil until nicely browned on all sides. Turn on one side and add the stock and simmer over low heat until tender. Turn a couple of times during roasting. Remove the chicken to a hot serving dish, either whole or cut into portions, and pour gravy over.

Serve with warm brown bread or rolls and a salad of raw, grated carrots, grated courgettes, shredded lettuce and coarsely chopped nuts in an oil and lemon dressing.

Stuffed Chicken

Stuffing a chicken is an excellent idea for several reasons – it makes the meat go further, and adds flavour and succulence. Below and overleaf are several tasty recipes for stuffed chicken which can be varied according to your own particular liking, for example by altering the spices and herbs included.

Stuffed Chicken
(serves 4)
Preparation time: about 25 min
Cooking time: 1–1¼ hr
Oven temperature (bottom shelf):
225–230°C, 430–450°F, Gas 7–8
Unsuitable for the freezer

*1 large fresh or frozen chicken
   (about 1.2kg or 2½ lb)
salt, pepper
butter, oil*

*300–400ml (½–¾pt) stock
For the stuffing:
2 slices of white bread
100ml (4fl oz) milk
50g (2oz) bacon
giblets from chicken, finely chopped
1 large or 2 small eggs
4–5 × 15ml tbsp (4–5tbsp) poppy
   seeds
salt, pepper*

1 Wipe the chicken thoroughly with a damp cloth. Rub the inside with salt and pepper.
2 Cut the bacon into small cubes and fry over moderate heat in oil or butter with the giblets for about 10 min. Cool. Cut the crusts off the bread and soak in warm milk. Mix the bread, bacon, giblets, eggs, poppy seed and seasonings.
3 Stuff the chicken and close opening (see illustrations below).
4 Brown the chicken on all sides in hot oil in a casserole. Season with salt and place in an ovenproof dish, breast side up. Roast the chicken in an oven preheated to the temperature indicated, basting with 1–2 × 15ml tbsp (1–2tbsp) melted butter and stock 2 or 3 times.
To test whether chicken is cooked, insert a metal skewer into the thickest part of the meat. If the juices run clear the chicken is cooked.

Stuffings for chicken can be very varied – bacon, giblets, vegetables, poppy seeds, nuts, etc, can all be used.

Cut the chicken into four and serve with gravy and boiled potatoes, rice or pasta. A mixed green salad makes a tasty accompaniment.

VARIATION
Instead of poppy seeds add 2–3 small onions cut into rings and 225g (½lb) coarsely chopped mushrooms. Alternatively, add 1 or 2 small, thinly sliced leeks and 1 or 2 finely chopped celery stalks.
For both variations, simmer the vegetables for 3–4 min in 15g (½oz) butter and 1 × 15ml tbsp (1tbsp) water, and with salt if necessary, before cooling and mixing into the stuffing.

NOTE
Using vegetables instead of poppy seeds increases the amount of stuffing. If there is some left over, put into small greased ramekins and roast it with the chicken for 20–30 min.

Stuffed Chicken
1 Stuff the chicken allowing a little space for the stuffing to expand during cooking.

2 Close the opening with cocktail sticks or skewers. Truss with thin string, to prevent the stuffing escaping.

Olive-stuffed Chicken (above)
(serves 4)
Preparation time: about 20 min
Cooking time: $1-1\frac{1}{4}$ hr
Oven temperature (bottom shelf):
225°C, 430°F, Gas 7
Suitable for the freezer, but will not
retain the full flavour

1 oven-ready chicken about 1kg (2lb)
salt, pepper
paprika
1 or 2 garlic cloves
200g (7oz) black or green olives
1 slice of white or brown bread
about 75g (3oz) butter
juice of 1 lemon
450–700kg (1–1½lb) potatoes
300–400ml (½–¾pt) stock

1 Wipe the chicken with a wet cloth
and then dry with absorbent paper.
Rub the inside of the chicken with
lemon juice, salt, pepper and paprika. Rub outside with a pinch of salt
and paprika. (NB the olives will give
the meat a salty flavour.)
2 Stone the olives and if necessary
rinse in cold water and chop coarsely. Mix with crushed garlic,
brown or white breadcrumbs, lemon
juice and about 40g (1½oz) diced
butter.
3 Stuff chicken with olive mixture
and close the opening with skewers.
Spread the surface with softened
butter and place in an ovenproof
dish.
4 Peel potatoes, cut into wedges and

season with a pinch of salt. Arrange
around chicken in dish. Add 100ml
(4fl oz) stock and roast in a preheated oven at the temperature indicated. Baste the chicken with stock
several times during roasting.
Remove the skin, and cut chicken
into neat pieces before serving.
Serve the roast potatoes and gravy
with the chicken, together with a
green salad.

TIPS
You can also roast chicken in roasting bag without adding any liquid,
or in a chicken brick with a little
liquid. The chicken can also be
cooked completely on top of the
cooker.

Chicken with Herb Stuffing

(serves 4)

Preparation time: about 20 min

Cooking time: about 1 hr

Oven temperature: 225°C, 425°F, Gas 7

Suitable for the freezer, but will lose some of its flavour

1 oven-ready chicken (about 1.1 kg or 2½lb)
salt, pepper
butter
200–300ml (7–10 fl oz) stock
100–200ml (4–7 fl oz) double or soured cream
2 × 15ml tbsp (2 tbsp) dry sherry (optional)
For the stuffing:
about 200g (7 oz) cottage cheese
1 egg, separated
100ml (4 fl oz) soured cream
3–4 slices crustless white bread
6–10 × 15ml tbsp (6–8 tbsp) finely chopped green herbs: chives,
parsley, chervil, tarragon
salt, pepper
garlic
lemon juice

1 Wipe the chicken inside and out with a damp cloth.

2 Mix the cottage cheese with egg yolk and soured cream. Mix in small cubes of white bread and finely chopped herbs and season with salt and pepper, crushed garlic and lemon juice. Set aside in a cold place for about 15 min then fold in the stiffly whisked egg white.

3 Stuff the chicken and stitch up the opening or close it with cocktail sticks and string. Rub the chicken with salt and pepper and place on a large piece of foil, greased with butter. Enclose the bird tightly with foil, sealing the edges together firmly.

4 Place in an ovenproof dish and roast for about 50 min. Turn back the foil for the last 10–15 min of roasting time, to brown the breast skin. Turn off heat and leave in the oven, loosely covered, for about 10 min.

5 Pour off the roasting juices, dilute with stock and boil with cream or soured cream. Season with salt and pepper and sherry, if liked.

Serve whole, and carve at the table. Meat juices, a green salad, rice or baked potatoes or butter toasted, garlic toasted bread cubes go very well with this.

NOTE The giblets can be used on another occasion or used for making stock with a beef bone, carrots, leek, celery, salt, peppercorns and a bouquet garni.

Chicken with Herb Stuffing is served with rice or roast potatoes and a green salad.

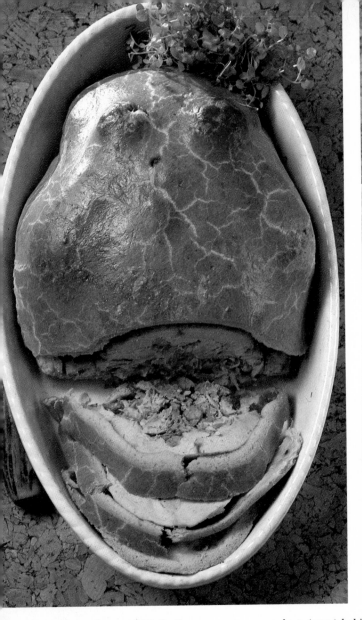

Festive Chicken

Baked Chicken Galantine
(serves 4)
Preparation time: 30–40 min
Cooking time: 1½ hr in all
Oven temperature (bottom shelf):
225 and 200°C, 425 and 400°F, Gas
7 and 6
Unsuitable for the freezer

1 oven-ready chicken (1kg or 2lb)
salt, pepper
butter
For the pastry:
250g (9oz) plain flour
½ × 5ml tsp (½tsp) salt
150g (5oz) butter

1 × 5ml tsp (1tsp) baking powder
1 egg + 1 egg for glazing
about 100ml (4fl oz) cold water
For the stuffing:
giblets from chicken
250g (9oz) mushrooms
3 slices crustless white bread
100ml (4fl oz) double cream
1 egg, 50g (2oz) walnuts
salt, pepper, butter

1 Bone the chicken (see pages 20–21) and season.
2 Mix all the pastry ingredients and knead to a smooth dough. Set aside in a cold place until required.
3 Chop the giblets and sauté with coarsely chopped mushrooms in 15–20g (1–1½oz) butter. Crumble bread and soak in cream. Mix with the giblets, mushrooms, egg, chopped walnuts and seasonings.
4 Stuff the chicken and close the opening with skewers. Brush surface with melted butter and place in an ovenproof dish, breast side uppermost. Brown for about 30 min at 225°C, 425°F, Gas 7. Season with salt and bake for a further 15 min at 200°C, 400°F, Gas 6. Leave to cool.
5 Roll out pastry to a rectangle and wrap chicken in it with the pastry join along the back of the bird. Place breast uppermost in an ovenproof dish. Brush with beaten egg and bake for about 45 min at 200°C, 400°F, Gas 6. Lower heat or cover with foil, if pastry browns too fast.

18

pour over chicken to cover it evenly.
4 Melt the butter for the sauce over low heat. Stir in flour and cook over low heat for 2 minutes until straw-coloured. Stir in warm stock and boil over low heat, stirring, for 10 min. Add the cream and boil for another 2 min. Cool, whisking from time to time. Thicken with whisked egg yolks and season. Pour sauce carefully over chicken until it is coated with an even layer of sauce. Refrigerate for 1½–2 hr. Serve cold, with lettuce leaves and sliced pâté.

Chicken with Green Stuffing
(serves 4)
Preparation time: about 30 min
Cooking time: about 1 hr
Oven temperature (bottom shelf): 250 and 200°C, 475 and 400°F, Gas 9 and 6
Suitable for the freezer, but will lose some of its flavour

1 oven-ready chicken weighing about
  1kg (2lb)
salt, pepper
butter
For the stuffing:
100ml (4fl oz) double cream
100g (4oz) crustless white bread
1–2 eggs
10–12 juniper berries
1 sprig of parsley
¾ × 5ml tsp (¾tsp) dried, crushed
  rosemary
½ × 5ml tsp (½tsp) dried, crushed
  sage
2–3 × 15ml tbsp (2–3tbsp) dry
  sherry or dry vermouth
salt, pepper

1 Bone the chicken (see page 20) and season to taste.
2 Make the stuffing: crumble the bread, soak in the cream and mix with egg, crushed juniper berries, chopped parsley, rosemary, and sage, wine and salt and pepper to taste. Allow to rest for about 10 min.
3 Stuff the boned chicken and close opening with metal skewers. Rub the surface with 40–50g (1½–2oz) softened butter and place breast side up in an ovenproof dish.
4 Brown in the oven for 20–25 min on high heat, season with a pinch of salt, lower the heat and roast for a further 30–40 minutes, brushing a couple of times with melted butter during cooking.

Coated Cold Chicken
(serves 4–6)
Preparation time: about 40 min
Cooking time (including stock): 3 hr in all + cooling
Unsuitable for the freezer

1 chicken weighing 1–1¼kg
  (2¼–2¾lb)
about 1kg (2lb) soup bones
salt, black peppercorns
vegetables and herbs
6g (¼oz) gelatine, optional
For the sauce:
50g (2oz) butter
4 × 15ml tbsp (4tbsp) plain flour
300–400ml (½–¾pt) stock
100ml (4fl oz) double cream
2–3 egg yolks

salt, white pepper
For the garnish:
lettuce leaves
100g (4oz) chicken pâté

1 Boil soup bones in a covered pan with a pinch of salt, a few peppercorns, vegetables and herbs (see page 29) for about 2 hr. Strain stock into a clean pan. Add the chicken and simmer, covered, for 30–40 min. Cool chicken in stock.
2 Skin chicken and place on serving dish. Skim fat from stock and cool.
3 If stock is not jellied when cold, add gelatine: sprinkle gelatine over cold water then dissolve in a bowl over a saucepan of boiling water. Mix with 200ml (7fl oz) stock and

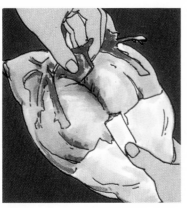

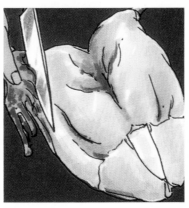

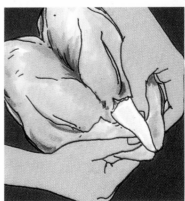

Removing Breast Bone

1 Prepare the chicken as on page 24 (steps 2–4), but do not remove wings. Insert a sharp knife close to the backbone and cut through and into the breast bone until you hear it crack.

2 Bend the breast bone upwards and break it away from the collar bone. Loosen the ribs clinging to the breast meat with your fingers. Cut away these ribs using a sharp pair of scissors or a knife.

3 Press your thumbs under the white piece of cartilage at the narrow end of the breast fillet and remove it.

Chicken Kiev (left)
(serves 2)
Preparation time: about 30 min
Cooking time: 15–20 min
Unsuitable for the freezer

Breast portions of 1 large chicken
salt, pepper
flour
1 egg
breadcrumbs
butter or oil
For the stuffing:
50–75g (2–3oz) butter
1 egg yolk

1 Remove bones from breast portions and make a pocket in each as illustrated. Soften the butter and mix with the egg yolk and a pinch of salt and pepper. Roll into a sausage shape on cling film, wrap, and refrigerate overnight or put into the freezer for 2 hours.

2 Cut the chilled butter in 2 lengthways and place in pockets of breasts. Close the opening with cocktail sticks or small skewers and coat in lightly seasoned flour. Dip chicken in beaten egg then coat in lightly salted breadcrumbs. Allow coating to dry.

3 Heat the butter in frying pan until golden brown or heat oil in a deep fryer. Fry fillets until brown and cooked right through. This will take 15–20 min in a frying pan or 12–15 min in the deep fryer. Drain on absorbent paper.
Serve with toast, deep fried parsley sprigs and a salad.

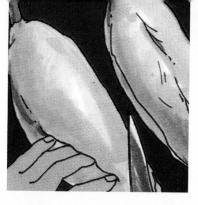

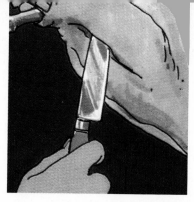

Stuffing and battering breast fillets

1 Halve the breast to make 2. Remove any ligaments, fat and so on.

2 Cut a pocket into the thickest side of the breast, but make sure you do not cut right through to the other side.

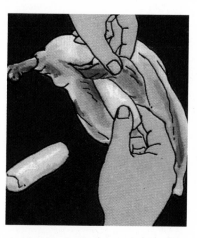

3 Fill the pocket with cold herb and garlic butter or any other stuffing. Squeeze edges together and close opening with small skewers.

4 Coat the stuffed breast in seasoned flour, then with beaten egg and breadcrumbs.

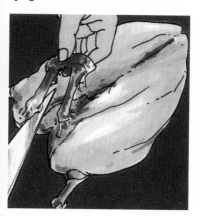

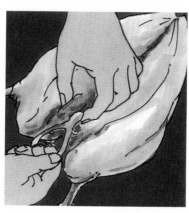

4 Run the point of a knife along the collar bone out to the joint that connects it with the shoulder blade and wish bone. Cut through joint and remove both bones on each side.

5 Pull wish bone upwards and remove it via the neck opening. Finally cut off the wings at the last joint.

TIPS
Chicken Roll
Chicken Kiev is often made using a rolled chicken breast, boned and beaten until flat. Prepare the butter as described, but do not chill. Spread the butter over the meat, then roll up and secure with string or cocktail sticks.
To double-coat the roll:
Coat first in lightly seasoned flour, then in egg white and bread crumbs and finally in egg white.

VARIATION
The butter filling can be seasoned with lemon juice, a little mustard or paprika.
You can also add finely chopped parsley or tarragon and garlic.

21

on each side in 25g (1oz) butter.
Season, then keep warm in heating
drawer or low oven.
3 Hard boil the egg, shell and chop.
Wash tomatoes and cut a cross in the
skin of each. Add more butter to the
pan and sauté tomatoes and chicory
for a couple of minutes. Arrange the
vegetables around the chicken and
keep warm. Add the breadcrumbs to
the pan and sauté, stirring, until
evenly golden. Season with a pinch
of salt and sprinkle over chicory
with chopped egg and parsley.
Serve immediately with sauté potatoes, chips or potato croquettes.
(You can buy frozen ones – follow
instructions on packet.) Deglaze the
frying pan with some of the cooking
water from endives. Season the
gravy with a little dry white wine
and hand separately in a gravy boat.

Roast Chicken Roll
(serves 6)
Preparation time: about 45 min
Cooking time: 60–70 min
Oven temperature (middle shelf):
200°C, 400°F, Gas 6
Suitable for the freezer, but will lose
a little of its flavour

*1 large, preferably fresh chicken
    weighing about 1.3kg (3lb)*
salt, pepper
paprika
butter
For the stuffing:
heart and liver from chicken
300g (11oz) minced pork
3–4 small onions
4 × 15ml tbsp (4tbsp) breadcrumbs
1 sprig parsley
salt
black pepper
paprika
1 small jar capers
1 × 5ml tsp (1tsp) mixed dried herbs
*2 × 15ml tbsp (2tbsp) brandy or
    fortified wine (sherry, Madeira or
    port)*

1 Bone the chicken breast as de-
scribed on pages 20–21 (steps 1–5).
Remove the wings and drumsticks.
Loosen the meat around joints with

Chicken Breasts with Chicory
(serves 2–3)
Preparation time: about 15 min
Cooking time: about 20 min in all
Unsuitable for the freezer

5–6 boned chicken breasts
4–5 medium chicory heads
salt, pepper
juice of ½ lemon
75–100g (3–4oz) butter
4 × 15ml tbsp (4tbsp) breadcrumbs
1 egg

small sprig parsley
2–3 tomatoes

1 Cut off the tough bases of the
chicory heads and as much as
possible of the thick tissue that ex-
tends into the heart. Remove any
dead leaves. Boil chicory for about
10 min in lightly salted water with
lemon juice added. Drain well.
2 Dry chicken well and beat lightly
with the palm of your hand. Fry
over medium heat for about 5 min

a sharp, pointed knife. Try to avoid slitting the skin and keep as much meat as possible inside the skin. Remove meat from drumsticks and wings. Place boned chicken flat, skin side down, cover with cling film then beat the meat carefully with the palm of your hand.

2 Rinse and dry liver and heart. Mince coarsely or use a food processor, but do not allow to become smooth. Peel and quarter onions and mince with the meat removed from drumsticks and thighs.

3 Mix minced chicken, giblets and onion with minced pork, breadcrumbs, chopped parsley, seasonings and dried herbs to taste. Drain the capers well and mix into the stuffing with the brandy or wine. Remove cling film from chicken. Spread stuffing over then roll into a thick, even sausage shape. Tie with thin string.

4 Brown chicken on all sides in 25g (1oz) butter in a flameproof casserole. Season with salt, pepper and paprika.

Place chicken in an ovenproof dish with a little butter and roast in oven at the temperature given.

Sprinkle a little chicken or vegetable stock over the chicken and turn it several times during cooking.

5 Transfer chicken to a carving dish, cover loosely and allow to rest for 10–15 min before carving into slices. Deglaze the ovenproof dish with a little stock to make some gravy. Serve the chicken hot with buttered boiled cabbage or other vegetables, boiled rice or mashed potatoes and gravy. It is also good cold, served thinly sliced and accompanied by French bread and a mixed green salad.

VARIATIONS

The minced stuffing can be varied in many ways. Try any of the following, mincing or chopping all the ingredients either finely or coarsely. Adjust the seasonings according to taste:

- 200g (7oz) cooked ham, giblets from chicken, 100g (4oz) mild, grated cheese, 2 slices crustless white bread, $\frac{1}{2}$ sprig parsley, $\frac{1}{2} \times 5ml$ tsp ($\frac{1}{2}$tsp) dried basil, 1 egg, 50–100ml (2–4fl oz) dry fortified wine, salt, pepper.

- 1 finely chopped pepper, 3–4 $\times$ 15ml tbsp (3–4tbsp) lemon juice, 1 small leek, 3 $\times$ 15ml tbsp (3tbsp) breadcrumbs, 3–4 $\times$ 15ml tbsp (3–4tbsp) strong stock, small bunch of chives, salt, pepper.

- 3 peeled onions, 8–10 stuffed olives, 1 onion, 75g (3oz) cooked rice, 1 $\times$ 15ml tbsp cornflour, 1 $\times$ 5ml tsp (1tsp) dried basil, small sprig of parsley, $\frac{1}{2}$ bay leaf, salt, pepper, paprika.

Roast Chicken Roll can be served hot with hot, cooked accompaniments, or cold with a green salad.

Chicken Pieces

Many recipes call for chicken joints or pieces. They are excellent for casseroles, deep frying, sautéeing, grilling or barbecueing.
Serve a whole wing joint or a large breast portion per person, a thigh joint or two drumsticks.

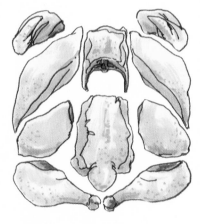

Jointing a Raw Chicken
1 A chicken can be jointed into 10 pieces or joints, some with more meat than others.

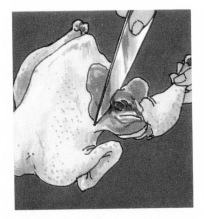

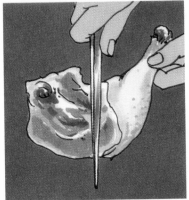

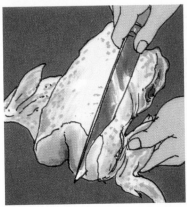

2 Place the chicken breast side up. Grip the drumstick firmly and cut through the skin, close to the body. Pull thigh away from body and cut through the joint at the top of the thigh.

3 Place the joint skin side down then cut through the joint between drumstick and thigh. There is no need to cut leg in two if chicken is small.

4 Press wing against the body of the bird. The shoulder joint will now be visible beneath the skin. Make an incision between the ball and socket parts of the joint.

Deep-fried Chicken Pieces

Allow 2 pieces of uncooked chicken per person.
Defrost frozen chicken slowly in the refrigerator then joint and dry well.
Preparation time: 15 min
Roasting time, for batter: 30 min
Cooking time: about 30 min
Unsuitable for the freezer

For the batter :
150g (5oz) plain flour
3 × 15ml tbsp (3tbsp) oil
1 egg
½–¾ × 5ml tsp (½–¾tsp) salt
about 200ml (7fl oz) water or non-alcoholic lager
oil or lard, for frying

1 Mix all the batter ingredients and allow to rest for about 30 min. Whisk lightly and add more liquid if necessary – the mixture should have the same consistency as pancake batter.
2 Heat oil or lard in a deep frying pan to 180–185°C, 82–85°F or until a crustless cube of white bread turns brown in 1 min.
3 Coat the chicken pieces in batter then turn in breadcrumbs. Place in the pan 2–4 pieces at a time and fry for 8–10 min. Turn several times with a lotted spoon or cooking tongs.
4 Remove chicken pieces and drain on absorbent paper. Sprinkle with salt. Do not fry too many chicken pieces at a time or the temperature will drop and the batter will soak up fat instead of forming a crisp coating

around meat.
Serve with freshly baked white bread, green salad or a cold, spiced soured cream sauce, or – as shown in the picture – with a casserole of hot mushrooms.

Jointing Fried or Boiled Chicken

To joint fried or boiled poultry, follow the steps given in the small illustrations.
To obtain boneless meat, first make an incision along the breast bone, and then run the knife along the ribcage down both sides.
In large birds the boneless breast meat is carved at an angle into two or more slices. You can then replace the slices on the carcass, along with the thighs and wings to make the bird look whole. Remember to remove the two small almond shaped pieces of meat located in cavities on either side of breast bone: many people think this is the most succulent meat on the bird.

Barbecued Chicken Pieces

Allow 3–4 fairly small pieces of un-cooked chicken per person. Thread on skewers and place pieces on the barbecue or grill pan and brush with well seasoned barbecue oil. Fry 8–10cm (3–4in) from coals or 12–15cm (5–6in) from the grill element. Turn and brush with bar-becue oil frequently. Sprinkle with salt when cooked.
Serve immediately with bread or boiled rice, mixed salad and cold

barbecue sauce or seasoned butter.
To vary the flavour of the meat, other spices and herbs can be added to the basic barbecue oil.
The basic recipe for barbecue oil is given below.

Barbecue Oil Mix

(basic recipe)
Mix 400ml (¾pt) olive oil with 1–2 × 15ml tbsp (1–2tbsp) wine vinegar or soy sauce, ½ × 5ml tsp coarsely ground black pepper in a screwtop jar and shake well.
Keep the jar in the refrigerator. When you use it, season a little of the oil according to taste. Try adding paprika, curry powder, ginger, tomato purée, grated onion, crushed garlic, crushed bay leaves, rose-mary, fennel, tarragon and/or thyme.

Chicken Casserole with Orange

(serves 4)
Preparation time: 15 min
Cooking time: 30–45 min
Unsuitable for the freezer

1 chicken weighing 900g–1kg (2–2½lb)
25g (1oz) butter
2 × 5ml tsp (2tsp) salt
6 whole cloves
2 × 15ml tbsp (2tbsp) tomato purée
200ml (7fl oz) chicken stock (made from a cube)
1 small orange
about 300g (11oz) frozen green beans
parsley

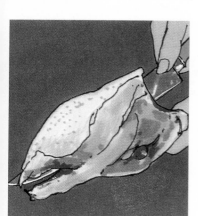

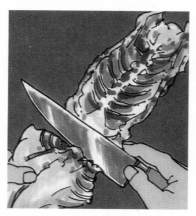

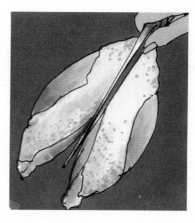

5 Place the knife inside the cavity of the bird and pierce one side between the shoulder joint and the rib cage. Cut through the ribs parallel to the back-bone. Repeat on the other side.

6 Pull the breast away from the back-bone. Cut off at the shoulder joints. Cut between these bones to detach the breast section. Cut the back into 2 at the point where the ribcage ends.

7 Place the breast skin side up and cut down through the breastbone and meat on one or the other side of its keel.

1 Divide the chicken into 6–8 pieces, dry well and fry in butter until golden.

2 Arrange the chicken in a casserole, sprinkle with salt and add the cloves, stock and tomato purée. Simmer for 30–45 min.

3 Defrost beans, cut into 2cm (½in) lengths and mix carefully with meat. Wipe orange, slice thinly and place in casserole. Warm over low heat for a couple of minutes. Sprinkle with finely chopped parsley and serve immediately. Mashed potatoes and a green salad taste particularly good with this.

Ginger Chicken

(serves 4)
Preparation time: about 20 min
Cooking time: about 45 min
Unsuitable for the freezer

1 chicken weighing 900–1000g
  (2–2¼lb)
salt, pepper
1 garlic clove
½–1 × 5ml tsp (½–1tsp) ground
  ginger
25g (1oz) butter
2 × 15ml tbsp (2tbsp) oil
50g (2oz) fresh ginger
  or 1 piece preserved ginger
1 green pepper
3–4 tomatoes
100–200ml (4–7fl oz) stock

1 Divide the chicken into 8 pieces. Dry well with a damp cloth. Rub with salt, pepper and crushed garlic, then sprinkle with ground ginger.

2 Heat butter and oil in a large shallow flameproof pan and sauté chicken on all sides. Peel fresh ginger and cut into slices or chop preserved ginger finely. Deseed the pepper and cut into thin strips. Peel and quarter the tomatoes. Add the vegetables to the pan.

3 Pour in a little stock and allow to simmer, covered, until the meat is tender. Add more stock as necessary and turn the chicken frequently. Uncover for the last 10–15 min of cooking time.

Serve straight from pan with boiled noodles tossed in garlic butter and a mixed, green salad.

Chicken in White Wine

(serves 4)
Preparation time: about 20 min
Cooking time: about 45 min
Unsuitable for the freezer

1 chicken weighing 900–1000g
  (2–2¼lb)
butter
salt, pepper
plain flour
4 small onions
400–600ml (¾–1pt) dry white wine
½ lemon
1 bay leaf
3 sprigs of parsley
2 celery leaves
225–450g (½–1lb) mushrooms
100–200ml (4–7fl oz) double cream

Left : Deliciously different Ginger Chicken, ideal with noodles and salad.

1 Quarter the chicken and wipe with a damp cloth. Coat with seasoned flour.

2 Sauté chicken pieces lightly on all sides in 25g (1oz) butter over medium heat. Peel and chop the onions and sauté in the casserole until transparent but not brown. Add 300–400ml ($\frac{1}{2}$–$\frac{3}{4}$pt) white wine and a bouquet garni, consisting of parsley, bay leaf, celery leaves and a strip of lemon zest. Simmer, covered until the chicken is tender.

3 Wipe the mushrooms and halve or slice. Sauté in 15–25g ($\frac{1}{2}$–1oz) butter and season with salt and lemon juice. Add 150–200ml (5–7fl oz) white wine and boil the mushrooms for about 2 min. Strain liquid from mushrooms and pour into the casserole. Remove bouquet garni.

4 Arrange the chicken pieces on a serving dish and keep warm. Boil up until it is reduced by half, then stir in the cream. Heat the mushrooms through and add to the casserole, taste and adjust seasoning. Pour some of the sauce over the chicken. Serve with the remaining sauce and rice seasoned with chopped herbs.

Above: Barbecued Chicken Pieces. Below: Chicken in White Wine.

Cheese-coated Spring Chicken
(serves 4)
Preparation time: about 20 min
Cooking time: about 30 min
Unsuitable for the freezer

2 spring chickens
$\frac{1}{2}$ lemon
about 100ml (4fl oz) oil
25–50g (1–2oz) breadcrumbs
100g (4oz) finely grated Gruyère
  cheese or other firm, mild cheese
basil, chopped parsley
butter
salt, pepper

1 Divide each chicken into 4 pieces. Wipe thoroughly with a damp cloth. Rub with the cut side of the lemon.

2 Mix breadcrumbs and grated cheese and season with a little salt, pepper and crushed basil. Brush chicken pieces with oil, coat with breadcrumb mixture and fry carefully in a mixture of butter and oil in a large frying pan over medium heat. Be careful not to burn the cheese coating.

Serve immediately, sprinkled with finely chopped parsley. French bread and a mixed salad and tomatoes go well with this dish.

Boiling Fowl

A boiling fowl cooked with interesting vegetables, spices and herbs is the ideal starting point for making stews and fricassées, but any kind of chicken can be cooked in the same way.
If you add a few meat bones to the pot, you get an even better stock perfect for soups and sauces.

Boiling Fowl
(serves 6)
Preparation time: about 20 min
Cooking time: $1\frac{1}{2}$–2 hr
Meat, vegetables and soup are suitable for the freezer if frozen separately

1 boiling fowl weighing about 2 kg
* (5lb)*
about 1kg (2lb) soup bones
salt, black peppercorns
3–4 carrots
1 large onion
1 whole clove
4 leeks
½ head of celery
1 parsley root (optional)
1 bay leaf
small sprig of parsley

1 Rinse the chicken and bones, if necessary, or wipe with a damp cloth.
2 Place bones and chicken in a casserole, add enough water to barely cover and bring to the boil. Remove all scum with a slotted spoon. Add 1 × 5ml tsp (1tsp) salt and 1 × 5ml tsp (1tsp) black peppercorns. Simmer, covered, over low heat for a good hour. Skim from time to time.
3 Clean all vegetables and make a bouquet garni consisting of the green part of the leek, celery leaves, bay leaves and parsley. Peel onion, press the cloves into it and place in casserole. Boil until chicken and

A boiling fowl, with beef, tongue, spiced sausages and vegetables makes a tasty, filling dinner in cold weather.

vegetables are tender. Remove the vegetables, bouquet garni, bones and chicken.
4 Strain stock and skim off excess fat. The stock can also be chilled and the solidified fat lifted off. Chicken fat has a strong, tasty flavour and can be used instead of or with butter in sauces and stews.
If you want to serve a clear chicken soup, it may be necessary to strain the liquid twice, the second time through a paper filter or a piece of damp muslin placed in a sieve.
5 To serve the meat and vegetables freshly cooked, keep warm, covered, in the stock. To serve the chicken, vegetables and soup later, keep them separately in the refrigerator or freezer. They can be safely stored in the refrigerator for 2–3 days, or even for 2–3 months.
When freezing, the chicken should be removed from the carcase, placed in a rigid container and covered with some of the stock before being sealed and frozen. Suggestions for using the chicken, vegetables and stock appear on the following pages.

Old-fashioned Chicken Soup with Meatballs
(serves 6)
Preparation and cooking time: as for Boiling Fowl (see recipe)
Soup, meat, vegetables and meat balls can be frozen separately

about 2l (3½pt) chicken stock
cooked meat from ¼–½ boiling fowl
2–3 boiled carrots
2 thin leeks
salt, parsley
For the meat balls:
250g (9oz) minced pork
salt, pepper
1 × 15ml tbsp (1tbsp) plain flour
1 small finely chopped onion
1 egg
100ml (4fl oz) single cream
For the dumplings:
100ml (4fl oz) water
75g (3oz) butter
75g (3oz) plain flour
½–1 × 5ml (½–1tsp) salt
2 eggs

1 Mix all the meat ball ingredients and shape with a spoon or piping bag. Place a few balls at a time in about 500ml (1pt) barely simmering chicken stock. Simmer for 4–8 min, depending on size, remove with

slotted spoon and dip quickly into cold water.

2 Bring the water for the dumplings to the boil with the butter. Sprinkle in the flour and mix well until dough is heated all the way through. Chill dough a little and mix in salt and lightly beaten eggs, a little at a time. The dough should be fairly firm. Shape small dumplings with a spoon or piping bag and lower into a saucepan of lightly salted, simmering water a few at a time. When the dumplings float to the surface, they are ready. Remove with a slotted spoon and place in cold water. Make the rest of the dumplings in the same way.

3 Heat the chicken stock until boiling and add strained stock from meat balls. Add thinly sliced leek rings and boil for 4–5 min then add small cubes of boiled carrot, small pieces of chicken meat and meat balls and dumplings. Heat through well, but do not allow to boil. Season with salt, if necessary. Serve sprinkled with parsley.

NOTE It is a good idea to make a double portion of meat balls and dumplings and freeze for later use.

Quick Chicken Soup
Basic Recipe
(serves 6–8)
Preparation time: about 15 min in all
Unsuitable for the freezer

2l (3½pts) chicken stock
25–40g (1–1½oz) butter
2–3 × 15 tbsp (2–3tbsp) plain flour
2 egg yolks
200ml (7fl oz) half cream
salt, white pepper

1 Boil stock. Mix softened butter and flour into a smooth paste and whisk into the stock a little at a time, until the soup is the correct consistency. Boil for a few minutes then add vegetables to taste (see Variations).

2 Whisk the egg yolks with the cream and some of the warm soup. Pour back into pan, whisking vigorously. Leave over a low heat and season to taste.

Boiling Fowl with Horseradish Cream served with boiled vegetables.

VARIATIONS
Asparagus Soup
Add 300–400g (11–14oz) asparagus spears including the liquid from the can. Season soup with 1–2 × 15ml tbsp (1–2tbsp) dry sherry or white wine. Serve with rolls.

Cauliflower Soup
Add small, lightly boiled sprigs of 1 medium cauliflower to the soup with some of the vegetable stock. Some of the cauliflower can be mashed before it is added to the soup. Serve with bread cubes fried in butter.

Mushroom Soup
Sauté 220–450g (½–1lb) cleaned, sliced mushrooms in 25g (1oz) butter, with the juice of ½ lemon. Allow mushrooms to boil in the soup for a couple of minutes before finishing with egg yolk and cream.

Flavour soup with lemon juice and serve with French bread or toast.

Boiling Fowl with Horseradish Cream
(serves 4)
Preparation and cooking time: as for Boiling Fowl (page 29)
Unsuitable for the freezer

½ cooked boiling fowl
300–400ml (½–¾pt) chicken stock
500–700g (1–1½lb) potatoes
boiled vegetables from chicken or
    mixed, frozen vegetables
salt
finely chopped parsley
about 200ml (7fl oz) double cream
2–3 × 15ml tbsp (2–3tbsp) grated
    horseradish
wine vinegar or lemon juice

1 Whip the cream, mix in grated horseradish and season with a couple of drops of wine vinegar or lemon juice and salt. Cover and refrigerate for about 1 hr.
2 Cut the chicken into pieces and heat through very slowly in some of the chicken stock.
3 Peel potatoes, quarter and boil in the remaining chicken stock, with a little salt until nearly tender. Cut the vegetables from the chicken stock into pieces and add to the pan with the potatoes for the last 5 min of cooking time.
Arrange the meat and vegetables on a hot serving dish. Pour over a little of the stock and sprinkle with parsley. Stir the horseradish cream and serve with the chicken.

Boiling Fowl with Cabbage
(serves 4)
Preparation and cooking time: as for Boiling Fowl (page 29)
Unsuitable for the freezer

½ cooked boiling fowl
1 small round or Savoy cabbage
400–500ml (¾–1pt) chicken stock
1 onion
45g (1½oz) butter
2 × 15ml tbsp (2tbsp) plain flour
1 egg yolk
100ml (4fl oz) single cream
salt, pepper, nutmeg

*Boiling Fowl with Cabbage,
served with a cream sauce.*

1 Remove outer leaves from cabbage, quarter and remove the stem. Boil in lightly salted water for about 5 min then transfer to a colander or sieve.
2 Skin and bone the chicken, then heat in some of the stock. Coarsely chop the cabbage, add the chopped onion and cook in 15g (½oz) butter and 100ml (4fl oz) stock for 6–8 min. Season to taste.
3 Melt the remaining butter, stir in the flour and cook for a few minutes until straw-coloured. Add the warm stock from the cabbage and meat, then whisk sauce until smooth and boil until heated through. Add lightly beaten egg yolk and cream. Keep just below boiling and season with salt, pepper and nutmeg.
4 Arrange chicken on a hot serving dish with the cabbage and pour some of the sauce over the meat.
Serve with remaining sauce and boiled potatoes.

31

Chicken Fricassée (above)
(serves 4)
Preparation and cooking time: as for
Boiling Fowl (page 29)
Suitable for the freezer but without
egg yolks and parsley

Meat from ½ cooked boiling fowl
2–3 carrots (from pot)
250g (9oz) frozen peas
1 sprig of parsley
For the sauce:
25g (1oz) butter
2 × 15ml tbsp (2tbsp) plain flour
200–300ml (7–10fl oz) chicken
  stock
100–200ml (4–7fl oz) single cream
1–2 egg yolks
salt, pepper

1 Cut meat into convenient pieces,
removing skin and bones. Heat meat
and boiled carrot pieces in the stock.
If using raw carrots, cut into small
cubes and boil until tender in some
of the stock. Add peas just before
carrots are tender.
2 Melt the butter for the sauce, stir
in the flour and allow to cook over
low heat, until straw coloured. Add
strained stock and whisk well. Boil
for a couple of minutes.
3 Whisk cream and egg yolks lightly
together and mix in some of the
warm sauce. Pour mixture back into
sauce and heat through without boiling point for a couple of minutes.
Season with salt and pepper.
4 Place meat and vegetables in

a dish, pour over the sauce and
sprinkle with parsley.
Serve warm with boiled potatoes.

Fricassée with Leeks
(serves 4)
Preparation and cooking time: as for
Boiling Fowl (page 29)
Suitable for the freezer without egg
yolk

Meat from ½ cooked boiling fowl
2 carrots (from pot)
2–3 leeks
1 onion
small sprig of parsley
small bunch of chives
1–2 tsp mild mustard
sauce as for Chicken Fricassée

1 Cut meat into convenient pieces and remove skin and bones. Heat meat and sliced carrots in some of the stock.

2 Wash and clean leeks. Cut into 2cm (½in) lengths. Cover leeks, finely chopped onion and finely chopped herbs in remaining stock.

3 Make the sauce as for Chicken Fricassée and season with mustard. Arrange meat and vegetables in a dish and pour over the sauce. Serve with potatoes or rice.

Chicken with Mushrooms (right)

(serves 4)
Preparation and cooking time: as for Boiling Fowl (page 29)
Unsuitable for the freezer

meat from ½ cooked boiling fowl
250g (9oz) mushrooms
15–25g (½–1oz) butter
juice of ½ lemon
salt
1 sprig of parsley
sauce as for Chicken Fricassée

1 Cut chicken meat into small pieces and remove skin and bones. Heat through in stock measured for the sauce.

2 Clean mushrooms, slice and sauté in butter for a couple of minutes. Season with salt and add lemon juice.

3 Make a sauce as for Chicken Fricassée and mix in meat, mushrooms and parsley. Serve hot with boiled potatoes.

Chicken with Cauliflower (right)

Boil cauliflower florets in lightly salted water and drain well. Make the sauce as for Chicken Fricassée and season with 2–3 × 15ml tbsp (2–3tbsp) grated cheese. Add meat and cauliflower in sauce, mix, then sprinkle with parsley.

Chicken and Asparagus

Heat the contents of 1 can asparagus in its own juice. Make a sauce as for Chicken Fricassée using the asparagus liquid for the sauce. Mix in the meat and asparagus in sauce and serve with French bread.

Chicken with Dill

Make a sauce as for Chicken Fricassée then add plenty of finely chopped dill and a little lemon juice. Add the meat and mix together.

Chicken Round the World

A country's home-grown produce, and its herbs and spices, give a national cuisine its typical flavour.
These chicken dishes, using Indian curry spices, Californian fruits and vegetables and Greek garlic and olives are just some of the many variations on this theme.

Indian Chicken
(serves 4)
Preparation (not including cooking of boiling fowl): about 20 min
Suitable for the freezer, but will lose some of its flavour

meat from ½ cooked boiling fowl
2 onions
25g (1oz) butter
2 cooking apples
½–1 × 15ml tbsp (½–1tbsp) curry powder
2 × 15ml tbsp (2tbsp) plain flour
salt, pepper
200–300ml (7–10fl oz) chicken stock
100–200ml (4–7fl oz) soured cream
2 mandarin oranges or tangerines
8–10 preserved, sour cherries

Californian Chicken Casserole

(serves 4)
Preparation time (without cooking chicken): about 25 min
Unsuitable for the freezer

meat from ½ cooked boiling fowl
1 courgette
1 carrot
1 small leek
½ cauliflower
2 stalks of celery
about 300ml (½pt) chicken stock
2 oranges
1 grapefruit
salt, pepper

1 Cut chicken meat into pieces and remove skin and bones. Wipe the courgette and slice fairly thickly, sprinkle with salt and leave in a cool place for 10–15 min.
2 Slice leek, peel carrot and slice lengthways. Divide cauliflower into florets and dice the celery.
3 Dry courgette slices on absorbent paper and boil in stock with other vegetables and the juice of 1 orange for about 5 min.
4 Peel the grapefruit and the other orange, removing as much of the white pith as possible. Pull the transparent membranes off segments. Put the fruit in a casserole with the vegetables and chicken meat. Heat well and season.
Serve with wholemeal bread or baked potatoes and a green salad.

VARIATION
Greek Chicken

Instead of carrot, cauliflower, oranges and grapefruit, add 1 chopped onion, 1–2 crushed garlic cloves, thin slices of 1 unpeeled lemon, 3–4 skinned, deseeded tomatoes and a few black or green olives, if liked. Serve with brown bread.

Above : Indian Chicken.
Right : Californian Chicken Casserole.

1 Cut the chicken meat into convenient pieces and remove skin and bones.
2 Sauté finely chopped onion in butter over low heat until soft and transparent. Add pieces of peeled apple and curry powder and cook for a couple of minutes. Add the flour, stir in chicken stock and boil, stirring, for about 5 min.
3 Mix in soured cream and season with salt and pepper. Add chicken meat, mandarin orange wedges and well-drained cherries and heat through until warm. Serve with rice and Mango Chutney.

Chicken in Aspic

Chicken in Spiced Aspic (below)
(serves 4)
Preparation time (without cooking chicken): about 20 min
Setting time: 3–4 hr
Unsuitable for the freezer

meat from ½ cooked boiling fowl
2 gherkins
15g (½oz) gelatine
200ml (7fl oz) chicken stock
200ml (7fl oz) white wine
1–2 × 15ml tbsp (1–2tbsp) red wine
  vinegar or lemon juice
salt, pepper
parsley
tarragon

1 tomato
1 bunch of radishes

1 Cut chicken meat into convenient pieces, remove skin and bones. Sprinkle gelatine over cold water and leave to soak for 5 min.
2 Dissolve gelatine in 100ml (4fl oz) stock over a saucepan of boiling water. Mix in the rest of the stock and white wine and season with salt and pepper, finely chopped herbs and wine vinegar. Leave in a cold place until nearly set.
3 Place chicken meat and sliced gherkins on a serving dish, pour over the aspic and leave in a cold place. Garnish with tomato wedges, radish flowers and parsley sprigs.
Serve cold as a luncheon dish with French or wholemeal bread.

Chicken in Aspic (right)
(serves 6)
Preparation time (without cooking the chicken): about 20 min
Setting time: 3–4 hr
Unsuitable for the freezer

breast from 1 cooked boiling fowl
15g (½oz) gelatine
200ml (7fl oz) chicken stock
100ml (4fl oz) dry white wine
1 can asparagus
salt, black pepper
2 cooked carrots
1 gherkin
2 eggs
2 tomatoes
about 100g (4oz) frozen peas

1 Sprinkle the gelatine into cold water and leave to soak. Dissolve in

100ml (4fl oz) warm chicken stock. Mix in remaining stock, wine and the liquid from the can of asparagus. Season with salt and pepper and leave in a cold place until nearly set. Hard boil the eggs.

2 Cut chicken meat into neat slices. Slice carrots, eggs, gherkin and tomatoes and asparagus.

3 Put a little chicken meat, vegetables and egg in a deep dish or mould. Spoon aspic over and allow to set completely. Continue in this way until all the ingredients have been used. If aspic sets too quickly, stir over low heat. The last layer should be completely covered with aspic. Leave dish in a cold place.

Serve as a first course, as part of a buffet, or as a dinner party dish accompanied by Spicy Mayonnaise.

Spicy Mayonnaise

(serves 6)

Mix about 200g (7oz) mayonnaise with 2–3 × 15ml tbsp (2–3tbsp) wine vinegar. Add 4–5 × 15ml tbsp (4–5tbsp) grated onion, 2 × 15ml tbsp (2tbsp) chopped capers, 1 × 15ml tbsp (1tbsp) finely chopped chervil, 1 × 15ml tbsp (1tbsp) chopped tarragon and 1 × 15ml tbsp (1tbsp) chopped parsley. Set aside in a cool place then season with salt, pepper and curry powder. Add a pinch of turmeric to give colour.

Chicken in Green Aspic

(serves 6)

Preparation time (without cooking chicken): about 20 min
Setting time: 3–4 hr
Unsuitable for the freezer

meat from ½ cooked boiling fowl
(or breast meat from 1 cooked
boiling fowl)
25g (1oz) gelatine
500ml (1pt) chicken stock
½ cucumber
salt, pepper
lemon juice
1 sprig of parsley
fresh or dried tarragon

1 Use only the light breast meat from the chicken and cut it into small cubes with a sharp knife. Sprinkle gelatine into cold water and leave for about 5 min. Wipe cucumber and cut into small cubes. Place cubes in a colander and sprinkle with salt.

2 Dissolve gelatine in 100–200ml (4–7fl oz) of chicken stock. Mix in remaining stock and finely chopped herbs. Season with lemon juice and salt and pepper.

3 Rinse cucumber cubes and shake off excess water. Rinse out a ring mould with cold water and pour a little aspic into the base. Allow to set. Fill mould with cucumber cubes and chicken meat and carefully pour the remaining aspic over. Cover and refrigerate until set.

4 Loosen the aspic around the edges and then dip the mould into hot water for a few seconds. Place serving dish on top of mould and turn over. Shake tin lightly until aspic is unmoulded. If the aspic mould is not central on the dish, push into place before removing the mould.

Serve as a starter, on a cold buffet or as a light supper with French bread and curried mayonnaise.

Curried Mayonnaise

Mix 150g (5oz) mayonnaise with 2–3 × 5ml tsp (2–3tsp) curry powder, the juice of ½ lemon and salt and pepper to taste. Stir in about 200ml (7fl oz) whipped cream and sprinkle with finely chopped cress.

A Chicken Salad Trio

Barbados Salad (left)
(serves 4)
Preparation time: about 15 min in all
Unsuitable for the freezer

about 250g (9oz) cooked chicken
3 small tomatoes
¼ cucumber
100g (4oz) mushrooms
lemon juice
2 slices of pineapple, fresh or
*   unsweetened canned*
a few lettuce leaves
For the dressing :
100g (4oz) mayonnaise
2–3 × 15ml tbsp (2–3tbsp) lemon
*   juice*
1 × 15ml tbsp (1tbsp) tomato purée
½ × 5ml tsp (½tsp) curry powder
salt, pepper
½ × 5ml tsp (½tsp) ground ginger
1–2 × 5ml tsp (1–2tsp) paprika

1 Cut skinned, boned chicken into strips. Wash tomatoes, cut into wedges and squeeze out pips. Wash cucumber and cut into thin strips. Sprinkle tomatoes and cucumber with a little salt.
2 Wipe the mushrooms, slice and sprinkle with lemon juice. Cut pineapple into pieces. Mix carefully.
3 Rinse lettuce leaves, place on individual dishes and arrange salad ingredients on top. Mix all the salad dressing ingredients and place spoonful on each portion.
Serve freshly made, with toast.

Normandy Salad
(serves 4)
Preparation time: about 20 min in all
Unsuitable for the freezer

200–300g (7–11oz) cooked chicken
1 lettuce
2 eggs
3 small tomatoes
100g (4oz) mushrooms
2–3 × 15ml tbsp (2–3tbsp) lemon
*   juice*
1 tart apple
10–12 stuffed olives
For the dressing :
100g (4oz) cream cheese

2–3 × 15ml tbsp (2–3tbsp) cream
salt, pepper
2–3 × 15ml tbsp (2–3tbsp) chives
and parsley

1 Cut the chicken into small cubes. Rinse lettuce leaves and dry in a tea towel. Shred the lettuce heart.
2 Hard boil the eggs and cut into thin wedges. Wash tomatoes, cut into wedges and sprinkle with a little salt.
3 Clean and slice mushrooms. Wash and cube apple. Toss mushroom slices and apple cubes in lemon juice. Slice olives.
4 Arrange the whole lettuce leaves on a dish. Mix the remaining salad ingredients and arrange on top.
5 Mash cheese with a fork and whisk with the cream until smooth. Season with salt and pepper and fresh, finely chopped herbs and pour over salad.
Serve freshly made with French bread and butter.

Salad Budapest
(serves 4)
Preparation time: about 15 min in all
Unsuitable for the freezer

about 200g (7oz) cooked chicken
about 100g (7oz) smoked ham, salt beef or tongue
1 stalk cooked celery
a few lettuce leaves
1 small tin asparagus spears
2 thin leeks or spring onions with tops
For the dressing:
3 × 15ml tbsp (3tbsp) mayonnaise
2 × 15ml tbsp (2tbsp) soured cream
1 × 15ml tbsp (1tbsp) tomato purée
1 × 15ml tbsp (1tbsp) lemon juice or wine vinegar
1 × 5ml tsp (1tsp) French mustard
salt, pepper
paprika

1 Cut the chicken, ham and celery into small cubes. Rinse lettuce and dry in a tea towel. Drain the asparagus and slice the leek or onions into rings.
2 Arrange lettuce leaves at the base of a salad bowl or a deep dish. Carefully mix the other salad ingredients together and place on top of lettuce. Mix the dressing and season. Pour dressing over salad and serve freshly made with brown bread and butter.

Above: Normandy Salad. Below: Salad Budapest.

39

Tasty Casseroles

All kinds of chicken are perfect for making colourful, tasty and tempting casseroles. If you are busy you can use a ready cooked chicken or chicken pieces instead of using uncooked poultry.

Paella (above)
(serves 6)
Preparation time: about 1 hr
Cooking time: 40–60 min in all
Unsuitable for the freezer

1 large oven-ready chicken
50–75 ml (2–3 fl oz) olive or other
good vegetable oil
100g (4oz) bacon
1 onion

200–300g (7–11oz) peeled prawns
1 can artichoke hearts, optional

1 Cut the chicken into 8–10 pieces
and dry them. Sauté lightly in oil
with thin bacon strips in a large,
deep pan.
2 Wash and clean peppers and cut
into strips. Peel onion and cut into
thin rings. Place vegetables in pan,
add crushed garlic and sauté until
well coloured.
3 Add lemon juice, saffron or turmeric, crushed bay leaves, salt,
pepper and rice. Stir carefully in pan
until rice is opaque. Add stock and
simmer, covered, for 15–20 min,
until chicken and rice are tender.
4 Mix in defrosted peas, artichokes
and well drained prawns and
mussels, reserving a few for garnish.
Heat through carefully, but do not
boil, or the shellfish will become
tough.
Serve Paella straight from the pan
and garnish with shellfish of your
choice, a few strips of pepper and
lemon wedges.
Serve with crisp, warm French
bread and butter.

Spiced Chicken Casserole
(serves 4)
Preparation time: about 15 min
Cooking time: 30–35 min
Suitable for the freezer, but will lose
some of its flavour

8 chicken drumsticks or 1 large
   chicken, jointed
25g (1oz) butter
1 × 15ml (1tbsp) oil
½–1 × 15ml tbsp (½–1tbsp) curry
   powder
salt, pepper
250g (9oz) button onions
1 green pepper
200ml (7fl oz) chicken stock
200ml (7fl oz) single cream
1 × 15ml tbsp (1tbsp) plain flour
watercress, tarragon

1 If necessary, cover chicken drumsticks loosely and defrost in refrigerator. Dry well and brown on all sides
in a casserole in butter and oil. Add
curry powder, season with salt and
pepper then remove meat.
2 Scald and peel onions. Wash and
deseed pepper and cut into cubes.
Sauté vegetables lightly in casserole

1 red and 1 green pepper
2 garlic cloves
juice of ½ lemon
¼–½ × 5ml tsp (¼–½tsp) saffron or
   turmeric
1 bay leaf
salt, black pepper
225g (8oz) long-grain rice
600–700ml (1–1½pt) chicken stock
200g (7oz) frozen peas
1 small can mussels in brine

Chicken with Bacon
(serves 4)
Preparation time: about 15 min
Cooking time: 35–45 min
Unsuitable for the freezer

a large oven-ready chicken
150g (5oz) thin bacon rashers
1 lemon
salt, pepper
paprika
rosemary
250g (9oz) mushrooms
butter
200ml (7fl oz) stock
150ml (¼pt) dry white wine

1 Cut the chicken into 6–8 pieces and dry well. Rub meat with lemon juice and leave for 10 min.
2 Reserve 2 bacon rashers and cut into 3. Dice the remainder and sauté in a knob of butter with the meat and season with salt, pepper, paprika and ½ × 5ml tsp (½tsp) dried, crushed rosemary. Lower the heat, add stock and simmer, covered, over low heat until tender.
3 Wipe mushrooms and sauté quickly in 15g (½oz) butter. Season with salt and lemon juice and add to casserole with the white wine.
4 Grill bacon slices lightly, roll up and place in casserole. Serve with parslied potatoes and a green salad.

Chicken Casserole with Rice
(serves 6)
Preparation time: 15–20 min
Cooking time: 40–45 min
Oven temperature: 180°C, 350°F, Gas 4
Suitable for the freezer, but will lose some of its flavour

2 large poussins or small oven-ready
  chickens
1 garlic clove
2 × 15ml tbsp (2tbsp) oil
25g (1oz) butter
100g (4oz) long-grain rice
250g (9oz) mushrooms
a few black olives, optional
2 × 5ml tsp (2tsp) salt
¼ × 5ml tsp (¼tsp) thyme
1 bay leaf
about 400ml (¾pt) chicken stock
1 small can of tomatoes
2–3 × 15ml tbsp (2–3tbsp) dry
  sherry

in remaining fat.
3 Lower the heat and return chicken to casserole. Add stock and simmer for about 20 min, or until chicken is tender.
4 Mix the flour and cream to a smooth paste and add 1–2 × 15ml tbsp (1–2tbsp) finely chopped watercress and tarragon. Add paste to casserole and simmer for a further 5 min.
Serve straight from the casserole or transfer to a hot serving dish and garnish with watercress. Serve with French bread and a green salad.

Chicken with Peaches
(serves 4)
Preparation time: 20 min
Cooking time: about 1 hr
Oven temperature: 190°C, 375°F, Gas 5
Unsuitable for the freezer

1 large chicken
butter
salt, black pepper
2 onions
2 carrots
50g (2oz) bacon rashers
¼ × 5ml tsp (¼tsp) thyme
1 bay leaf
300ml (½pt) peach juice

2 × 5ml tsp (2tsp) cornflour
8 canned peach halves
parsley

1 Cut chicken into 6–8 pieces. Season with salt and pepper, fry until golden in butter and place in an ovenproof casserole.
2 Peel onions and carrots and slice thinly. Sauté onion and carrot slices for a couple of minutes in a knob of butter. Remove rinds and fat from bacon, cut into thin strips and sauté lightly. Place vegetables and bacon in casserole.
3 Add thyme, bay leaf and peach juice from can (if less than required, add water). Cover with a tightly fitting lid and cook in preheated oven for about 1 hr, or until chicken pieces are tender.
4 Remove casserole from oven. Thicken sauce with cornflour worked to a paste in a little cold water. Simmer for a couple of minutes, then taste and adjust seasoning, if necessary.
Slice 4 peach halves and add to casserole. Garnish with the remaining peaches and a few parsley sprigs. Serve warm with boiled rice or French bread and a tossed green salad.

1 Joint chickens (see pages 24–5). Fry until golden in oil and butter with crushed garlic added.

2 Add rice, olives, thyme and bay leaf, stock, tomatoes, mushrooms and sherry. The liquid should cover the rice completely.

3 Cover with a tightly fitting lid or double layer of foil and cook in a preheated oven until the chicken is tender. Remove bay leaf. Serve with French bread and a green salad.

French Chicken Casserole
(serves 4–5)
Preparation time: about 30 min
Cooking time: about 20 min in all
Unsuitable for the freezer

1 large cooked chicken
1 aubergine
2 courgettes
¼ cucumber
1 green pepper
3 tomatoes
2 onions
1–2 garlic cloves
oil
salt, pepper
200–300ml (7–10fl oz) chicken stock
tomato purée
lemon juice
parsley
rosemary
basil
marjoram

1 Divide chicken into 10–12 pieces and remove skin and bones.

2 Wash and clean all vegetables and slice or cut into wedges. Put aubergine, courgette and cucumber in a colander, sprinkle with coarse salt, cover with a plate and leave for 15–20 min. Dry with absorbent paper.

3 In a deep casserole, sauté finely chopped onion and crushed garlic in 3–4 × 15ml tbsp (3–4tbsp) oil. Add all vegetables, except tomatoes, and heat through.

4 Add tomatoes and stock, then season with tomato purée, lemon juice, salt and pepper and fresh or dried, crushed herbs to taste.

Simmer for 10–15 min cooking the chicken for the last 5 min cooking time.

Serve with French bread or brown bread and butter.

Filling French Chicken Casserole needs only simple accompaniments. Serve it with French bread and a green salad.

Coq au Vin Blanc

(serves 4–6)
Preparation time: about 30 min
Cooking time: 50–60 min in all
Suitable for the freezer, but will lose some of its flavour

1 small boiling fowl or large oven-
    ready chicken
100g (4oz) bacon
oil
salt, pepper
10–12 shallots
    or button onions
250g (9oz) mushrooms
100–200ml (4–7fl oz) stock
300–400ml (½–¾pt) dry white wine
40g (1½oz) butter
1 × 15ml tbsp (1tbsp) plain flour
finely chopped parsley

1 Wipe chicken with a damp cloth. Cut into pieces (see pages 24–5). Peel onions and dice bacon.
2 Sauté chicken, if necessary half at a time, then transfer to a large casserole or deep pan. Season with salt and pepper and add stock. Cover with a tightly fitting lid and simmer over low heat for 30–40 min.
3 Wipe and quarter mushrooms. Sauté in 25g (1oz) butter, season with salt and add white wine. Bring to the boil then thicken meat juices with butter and flour (see small pictures). Simmer mushroom sauce for a few minutes.
4 Pour mushroom sauce over chicken pieces and heat well. Season with salt and pepper if necessary, then sprinkle with plenty of finely chopped parsley.
Serve with rice or boiled new potatoes.

NOTE This dish comes from Alsace in France. Correctly, you should use white wine from this district when making this dish, since it has a light, characteristic flavour. Any dry white wine will, however, be perfectly adequate.

Chicken à la King

(serves 6)
Preparation time: about 20 min
Cooking time: about 15 min
Unsuitable for the freezer

meat from 1 cooked boiling fowl or 1
    large chicken
1 red and 1 yellow pepper
40g (1½oz) butter
3 × 15ml tbsp (3tbsp) plain flour
500g (1lb 2oz) mushroms
juice of 1 lemon
1 can tomatoes
200ml (7fl oz) chicken stock
250ml (9fl oz) double cream
3 egg yolks
salt, pepper
paprika
2–3 × 15ml tbsp (2–3tbsp) medium
    sherry

1 Cut chicken into small, even pieces. Deseed and cut peppers into small dice.
2 Wipe mushrooms and sauté in 25g (1oz) butter, season with salt and squeeze lemon juice over. Turn off heat.
3 Sauté pepper cubes in remaining butter in a large casserole for about 5 min. Stir in flour and cook, stirring, for a few minutes until straw-coloured. Add tomatoes and stock. Cook, stirring constantly, until thick and smooth then simmer for 6–8 min.
4 Add chicken and mushrooms to casserole and bring to the boil. Whisk egg yolks with cream, stir into casserole and heat through without boiling. Season dish with salt, pepper and paprika and stir in sherry.
Serve with sweetcorn, French bread and a green salad.

Coq au Vin Blanc
1 Divide chicken into suitable portions (see pages 24–5).

2 Sauté chicken pieces and place in a deep pan or casserole, with bacon and whole shallots or onions.

3 Work 25g (1oz) softened butter and 1 × 15ml tbsp (1tbsp) plain flour together to make a smooth paste.

4 Whisk into the boiling meat juices a little at a time. The sauce should not be too thick.

Coq au Vin Blanc is French cooking at its best.

Roast Turkey

Turkey meat is light in colour, easy to digest and lean – and has a flavour to everyone's taste.

Roast turkey, with or without stuffing, satisfies even the most discriminating palate.

Stuffed Turkey
(serves 6–8)
Preparation time: about 40 min
Defrosting time: 1½–2 days
Cooking time: about 2 hr
Oven temperature (bottom shelf):
190 and 250°C, 375 and 475°F, Gas
5 and 9
Bottom grid in the oven
Suitable for the freezer, but will lose
a little of its flavour

1 small frozen turkey weighing
  2–2½kg (4½–5¾lb)

salt, pepper
butter
300–400ml (½–¾pt) dry white wine
about 200ml (7fl oz) soured cream
soy sauce
1–1½kg (2¼–3lb) potatoes
1 sprig of parsley
¼ lemon
For the stuffing:
turkey giblets
250g (9oz) minced pork
2 crustless slices white bread
150ml (¼pt) dry white wine
75–100g (3–4oz) hazelnuts

1–2 small onions
1 egg
salt, pepper
thyme

1 Wipe the oven-ready turkey with a damp cloth. Rub the inside with a sliced lemon, and season with salt and pepper. Cover turkey loosely and defrost slowly in refrigerator.

2 Chop giblets finely and mix with minced pork, bread soaked in white wine, chopped nuts, grated onion, egg, salt and pepper to taste and a generous pinch of dried thyme.

3 Stuff body cavity of turkey with most of stuffing, then stuff remainder into neck cavity.
Loosen neck skin from upper part of breast with your fingers.
Pull neck skin down under the bird, twist wingtips over and fasten with skewers. Close opening with grill skewers and rub turkey with salt and 25–40g (1–1½oz) butter.

4 Place turkey in an ovenproof dish, add white wine and cover with roasting film or foil. Cook in the oven at 190°C, 375°F, Gas 5 for about 30 min. Remove roasting film or foil. Pour off meat juices. Meanwhile, turn the oven up to 250°C, 475°F, Gas 9.
Return the turkey to the oven for the remaining roasting time, turning it frequently so that it is well browned on all sides.

5 Boil up juices from pan and add soured cream, a little at a time until

Stuffed Turkey is served here with a wine and soured cream sauce and butter-fried potatoes.

the sauce has the correct consistency, bringing it to the boil between each addition. Season with salt and pepper and add a few drops of soy sauce.

6 Well in advance, boil potatoes in their jackets then rub off skins. Heat 100g (4oz) butter in a saucepan or casserole until golden, but not brown. Add finely chopped parsley and 1–2 × 5ml tsp (1–2tsp) lemon juice then sauté potatoes over low heat until cooked through. Season with salt.
Serve stuffed turkey with sauce, potatoes and a salad, consisting of finely shredded chicory, apple cubes and deseeded grape halves, sprinkled with lemon juice. Remove some of the stuffing from the turkey when serving.

VARIATIONS
Rice Stuffing
(sufficient for a turkey weighing about 2kg or 4½lb)
1 chicken or turkey liver
1 small onion
50g (2oz) blanched almonds
2 × 15ml tbsp (2tbsp) finely chopped parsley
50g (2oz) raisins
about 100g (4oz) boiled rice
salt, pepper
25g (1oz) butter
egg (optional)

Finely chop liver, onion and almonds. Mix with rice, raisins, parsley, salt and pepper. Melt butter and mix into stuffing. If necessary, add enough lightly beaten egg to give the correct consistency.

Apricot Stuffing
(sufficient for a turkey weighing about 2kg or 4½lb)
225g (8oz) canned or
   100g (4oz) dried apricots
1½–2 × 5ml tbsp (1½–2tsp) ground ginger
about 100g (4oz) crustless white bread
about 50g (2oz) lard
1 large egg
salt, pepper

Soak dried apricots in water overnight. Finely chop apricots and lard, crumble bread and mix together to make a smooth stuffing.
Season with salt, pepper and ginger, and other spices of your choice.

Sausage and Apple Stuffing
(sufficient for a turkey weighing about 4½kg or 10lb)
about 500g (1lb 2oz) cooked pork boiling sausage
butter, for frying
3 firm apples
1 onion
2 stalks of celery
about 200g (7oz) crustless white bread
2 eggs
1½ × 5ml tsp (1½tsp) salt
½ × 5ml tsp (½tsp) pepper

Dice sausage and sauté lightly in about 50g (2oz) butter. Remove sausages and add finely chopped onion, celery and apple cubes to the pan. Cook over low heat until apples and vegetables are tender.
Crumble bread and beat eggs lightly. Mix all ingredients together.

Stuffed Turkey
1 Assemble all the ingredients to be used.

2 Pour meat juices into a pan and add cream gradually, bringing to the boil between each addition.

3 Fry boiled potatoes in heated butter, with chopped parsley and lemon juice added.

Port-marinated Turkey

(serves 6–8)
Preparation time: about 40 min
Marinating time: 8 hr for fresh turkey, 1½–2 days for frozen turkey
Cooking time: about 2 hr
Oven temperature (bottom shelf):
190 and 250°C, 375 and 475°F, Gas 5 and 9
Suitable for the freezer, but will lose a little of its flavour

1 small oven-ready turkey weighing
    2–2½kg (4½–5¾lb)
salt, pepper
butter
200ml (7fl oz) double cream
For the marinade:
½ bottle medium dry port
For the stuffing:
turkey giblets
300g (11oz) minced veal and pork
    or the same weight minced pork
1 slice crustless white bread
100ml (4fl oz) double cream
1 egg
50g (2oz) chopped walnuts
salt, pepper
To garnish:
2 × 15ml tbsp (2tbsp) sugar
50ml (2fl oz) water
50g (2oz) walnuts

1 Wipe turkey with a damp cloth and place breast side downwards in a dish with port. Cover and leave in a cool place for 8 hr. Frozen turkey can be defrosted in the port. Season

Left: Chestnut-stuffed Turkey.
Right: Port-marinated Turkey.

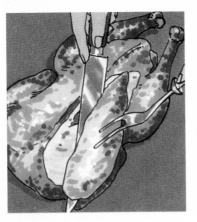

Carving a Turkey
1 Cut along breastbone and slice away meat, cutting at an angle.

2 Cut breast meat into slices 1–1½cm (½–¾in) thick as shown. Cut off the meat from the other breast.

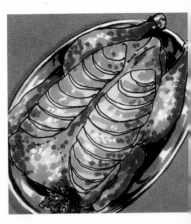

3 Replace slices on bird and cut off thighs. These can also be sliced down the bone.

defrosted turkey with salt and freshly ground black pepper.

2 Mix the minced meats, bread soaked in cream, egg, nuts and salt and pepper. Stuff the body and neck cavities of the turkey and close openings with grill skewers. Season turkey with a little more salt and about 25g (1oz) softened butter and roast with marinade as for Stuffed Turkey (pages 46–7). Dish up the turkey.

3 Boil up the juices add cream, and boil until smooth. Season with salt and pepper. Put brown sugar in a frying pan and cook with water until it looks like caramel. Add coarsely chopped nuts and stir mixture for 2 min over low heat. Pour over the roast turkey.

Serve with sauce, parslied potatoes and a salad made of apple wedges and walnuts coated in a dressing of equal parts of mayonnaise and whipped cream, seasoned with lemon juice.

Chestnut-stuffed Turkey
(serves 6–8)
Preparation and cooking time: as for previous recipe
Suitable for the freezer, but will lose some of its flavour

1 small oven-ready turkey weighing
  2–2½kg (4½–5¾lb)
salt, pepper
butter
300–400ml (½–¾pt) dry red wine
For the stuffing :
turkey giblets
250g (9oz) minced pork
1 onion
butter
500g (1lb 2oz) chestnuts
about 300ml (½pt) stock
250g (9oz) mushrooms
2 slices crustless white bread
1 glass red wine
1 egg
salt
pepper
thyme

1 Rub turkey with salt and pepper.
2 Make an incision in the pointed end of each chestnut and boil for about 15 min in unsalted water. Peel then boil in stock in a covered pan for 30–40 min until tender. Wipe mushrooms and sauté in 15g (½oz) butter and season with salt.
3 Chop giblets and about half the chestnuts finely and mix with minced meat, grated onion, about 100g (4oz) chopped mushrooms sautéed in butter, egg, seasonings and bread soaked in red wine.
4 Stuff body and neck cavity of turkey then rub the bird with salt and 15–25g (½–1oz) softened butter. Roast turkey with red wine as for Stuffed Turkey, pages 46–7.
5 Pour off cooking juices and heat the remaining chestnuts and mushrooms in it. Place turkey on a hot serving dish, garnish with warm chestnuts and mushrooms.
Serve with a gravy of cooking juices and roast or baked potatoes.

Salt Turkey and Pea Soup

On a cold winter's day a thick pea soup containing meat such as pork is both warming and sustaining.
Instead of the traditional split peas, pork and ham, this recipe calls for split peas, turkey and ham.

Salt Turkey and Pea Soup
(serves 8–10)
Preparation time: about 40 min
Salting time, if necessary: $1\frac{1}{2}$ days
Soaking time for peas: about 2 hr
Cooking time: about 2 hr in all
Meat and soup are suitable for the freezer if frozen separately

1 turkey weighing 2–2$\frac{1}{2}$kg (4$\frac{1}{2}$–5$\frac{3}{4}$lb)
1–1$\frac{1}{2}$kg (2$\frac{1}{4}$–3lb) lean belly pork
about 1kg (2$\frac{1}{4}$lb) fresh ham bones
500g (1lb 2oz) carrots
1 head celery
1 parsnip (optional)
1 sprig of parsley
4 leeks
500g (1lb 2oz) button onions
500g (1lb 2oz) yellow split peas
black peppercorns
For 2 bouquets garnis:
green part of leek
leaves of celery
top of parsley
5–6 sprigs of thyme
2 bay leaves

1 Make a boiling brine using 6 litres (10$\frac{1}{2}$pt) water, 1kg (2$\frac{1}{4}$lb) coarse sea salt, 200g (7oz) granulated or icing sugar, 3 bay leaves, 4 sprigs of thyme and 1–2 sliced garlic cloves. Set aside until cold, then pour over turkey and pork, to cover both completely. Cover and leave in a cool place for 1$\frac{1}{2}$ days.

Filling yellow pea soup, salt turkey and ham, is wonderful winter fare. Although it may seem time consuming to make, in fact this casserole will look after itself for most of the time. Any left-over meat or soup can be frozen.

2 Remove meat from brine and tie pork into a neat shape. Place turkey and pork (belly plus ham bones) in separate pans, barely cover them with cold, unsalted water and bring to the boil. Skim and add 1 × 5ml tsp (1tsp) black peppercorns and a bouquet garni to each pan. Cover and simmer over low heat for about 1$\frac{1}{2}$ hr.
3 Meanwhile, clean all vegetables and slice all but the onions. Remove bouquets garnis and ham bones and peppercorns if possible. Place vegetables in the pan with the most space and simmer for the last 15–20 min of cooking time.
4 Rinse peas in cold water and add to one pan. Add enough meat stock to cover peas completely. Simmer over low heat for $\frac{1}{2}$–$\frac{3}{4}$ hr depending on the degree of mushiness you prefer. Very soft peas can be beaten to form a smooth purée.
5 Remove meat and keep warm. Mix the vegetables with the peas and add enough stock from meat to give soup the correct consistency. Taste and season with salt, if necessary.
Place meat on a hot serving dish and serve meat and soup at the same time, with boiled potatoes, mustard and/or brown bread.

TIP
To make the meat go further, add a pork sausage to the turkey and pork. Cook raw sausages in stock with the vegetables, or heat ready boiled pork sausages in stock.

VARIATION
You can use a goose in place of a turkey, but the cooking time will then be 2–2$\frac{1}{2}$ hr. For a salt duck, the cooking time is about 1$\frac{1}{2}$ hr.

Turkey for Every Occasion

Turkey is quick and easy to prepare, as the recipes here and overleaf prove conclusively.
And any left-overs can be used in delicious casseroles or soups.

Turkey Roll
(serves 4)
Defrosting time (if necessary): 10–12 hr
Preparation time: about 15 min
Cooking time: about 1 hr
Meat is suitable for the freezer

about 500g (1lb 2oz) boneless turkey
  meat (breast, thigh, frozen if
  liked)
salt
black peppercorns
3 carrots
½ head celery or ¼ celeriac
bay leaves
1 leek
½ cauliflower
For the sauce :
2 eggs
2 × 5ml (2tsp) English mustard
200ml (7fl oz) oil
wine vinegar
salt
1 bunch of chives

1 Remove bones from 2 or 3 turkey
thighs or breast pieces, form meat
into a roll shape and tie with thin
string. (You can also boil the meat
with the bones in, but this makes the
carving more difficult.)
2 Place the meat, (fresh or defrost-

Tasty, quick and easy to make. Left :
Turkey Roll with vegetables. Below :
Delicious Turkey Soup with a
sprinkling of green chives.

ed) in a pan, barely cover with water,
and bring to the boil. Skim well and
add 1–2 × 5ml tsp (1–2tsp) salt, 6
black peppercorns and a bouquet
garni made from the green part of
the leek, bay leaves and leaves from
celery. Simmer, covered over low
heat for 35 min.
3 Meanwhile clean the vegetables
and cut into fairly large pieces.
Remove bouquet garni, add vegetables to stock and cook until tender.
Remove meat and vegetables and
keep warm.
4 While meat and vegetables are
boiling make the sauce : hard boil the
eggs and cool under cold running
water. Shell, halve and remove
yolks. Rub yolks through a fine
meshed sieve and mix with mustard.
Add oil, at first drop by drop, then in
a steady stream, stirring vigorously.
The sauce should have the same
consistency as mayonnaise. Season
with a few drops of wine vinegar,
salt, and finely snipped chives. The
egg whites can be finely chopped
and mixed into the sauce.
Slice meat and place on a warmed
serving dish with the vegetables.
Serve with the egg sauce and crisp
French bread or boiled potatoes.

Turkey Soup
(serves 4)
Preparation time: about 10 min
Cooking time : 10–12 min
Unsuitable for the freezer

200–300g (7–11oz) cooked turkey
  meat without skin and bones
about 1l (1¾pt) turkey or chicken
  stock
20g (¾oz) butter
2 × 15ml tbsp (2tbsp) plain flour
2 egg yolks
100ml (4fl oz) cream
salt, pepper
1 bunch of chives

1 Cut meat into neat, even-sized
pieces and heat in an uncovered pan
in about 100ml (4fl oz) stock over
low heat.
2 Bring the rest of the stock to the
boil and thicken with a butter and
flour paste, whisking vigorously as it
is added. Simmer for 8–10 min.
3 Remove soup from heat. Whisk
egg yolks with cream and mix with
some of the soup. Pour back into
saucepan and keep soup on the
verge of boiling. Season with salt,
pepper and finely snipped chives.
Add turkey meat and serve.

Swiss Turkey can also be made from any turkey left-overs.

remove any stalks. Defrost frozen spinach in a sieve, to allow excess water to drain away. Chop spinach coarsely, sauté in butter for a couple of minutes and season with salt and nutmeg.

3 Cut ham slices in half and place half in the base of a greased oven-proof dish. Spread spinach on top, followed by turkey meat and cover with the remaining ham. Cover with cheese slices and pour in chicken stock and wine. Cook in a preheated oven for about 30 min or until the cheese is golden and the dish is heated through.

Serve straight from the oven with French bread and a green salad.

TIPS

This dish can also be made from left-over boiled or roast turkey. Cut meat into suitable pieces and remove skin, if any. Follow the recipe, but do not brown the meat in butter.

Turkey Kebabs
(serves 4)
Preparation time: about 15 min
Cooking time: about 20 min
Unsuitable for the freezer

400–500g (14oz–1lb 2oz) boneless turkey meat (for instance breast meat)
200–300g (7–11oz) thick bacon rashers
100ml (4fl oz) oil
juice of ½ lemon
salt, pepper
thyme

1 If necessary defrost frozen meat slowly in refrigerator. Dry, then cut into fairly large cubes. Cut bacon into pieces about the same size as turkey cuts. Place turkey and bacon alternatively on individual skewers.
2 Mix a barbecue oil consisting of oil, lemon juice, 1 × 5ml tsp (1tsp) salt, ½ × 5ml tsp (½tsp) pepper and

Swiss Turkey
(serves 4)
Preparation time: about 25 min
Cooking time: about 30 min in all
Oven temperature (middle shelf):
225°C, 425°F, Gas 7
Unsuitable for the freezer

400–600g (14oz–1¼lb) boned turkey breast meat
salt, pepper
nutmeg
butter
about 500g (1lb 2oz) fresh spinach

or 1 large packet frozen spinach
4 slices cooked ham
200ml (7fl oz) chicken stock
150ml (¼pt) dry white wine
4 slices Gruyère cheese or other mild, high fat cheese

1 If necessary, defrost meat slowly in the refrigerator. Beat turkey breasts flat and cut into four. Rub meat with a little salt and pepper and brown lightly on both sides in butter.
2 Rinse fresh spinach well and

Right : Delicate and delicious turkey meat and bacon combine well in kebabs. Below : Turkey Ragoût is easily made from left-overs.

$2 \times 5ml$ tsp (2tsp) fresh or $\frac{1}{2} \times 5ml$ tsp ($\frac{1}{2}$tsp) dried thyme. Shake well.
3 Brush meat with barbecue oil and place on barbecue grid 15cm (6in) from glowing coals or a grill pan the same distance from a heated grill. Turn frequently and brush it with oil at each turning.
Serve with hot, baked potatoes or bread and butter and with cooked vegetables or a tasty salad.

Turkey Ragoût
(serves 4)
Preparation time: about 15 min
Marinating time: 30 min
Cooking time: 8–10 min
Suitable for the freezer, but will lose a little of its flavour

300–400g (11–14oz) cooked turkey meat, without skin and bone
1 green, 1 yellow and 1 red pepper
100ml (4fl oz) dry white wine or turkey or chicken stock
1 × 15ml tbsp (1tbsp) lemon juice
250g (9oz) mushrooms
20g ($\frac{3}{4}$oz) butter
1$\frac{1}{2}$ × 15ml tbsp (1$\frac{1}{2}$tbsp) plain flour
300ml ($\frac{1}{2}$pt) turkey stock
100 ml (4fl oz) double cream
salt, white pepper

1 Cut turkey meat into thin strips. Wipe and deseed peppers and cut into strips. Place pepper strips in a dish with the meat and pout over white wine or stock and lemon juice. Leave in a cool place for about 30 min.
2 Wipe mushrooms and sauté carefully in butter. Sprinkle with flour and sauté for a couple of minutes without browning. Add hot stock and simmer for about 5 min, stirring from time to time.
3 Add cream, meat and peppers, including marinade and boil for 2–3 min. Season with salt and pepper. Serve piping hot with boiled rice and a mixed green salad.

Roast Duck on the Menu

Roast duck stuffed with rice or fruit makes perfect party fare. Cold roast duck makes an attractive centrepiece for a cold buffet, or you can turn your duck into an unusual pâté.

Roast Duck with Herbs
1 Rub inside of duck with salt, pepper and parsley. Stuff with soaked prunes and apple wedges.

2 Trim neck skin over towards the back and fasten securely with metal skewers. Rub duck skin with salt.

3 Towards end of cooking time turn heat up to 250°C, 475°F, Gas 9. Baste with a little water and sprinkle with parsley to give a crisp skin.

4 Mix flour with a little water to a creamy consistency. Stir into gravy and boil sauce for a couple of minutes.

Roast Duck with Herbs
(serves 4)
Preparation time: about 30 min
Cooking time: about 2 hr
Oven temperature (bottom shelf):
200°C, 385°F, Gas 5
Suitable for the freezer, but will lose a little of its flavour

1 oven-ready duck with giblets
  weighing 2–2½kg (4½–5lb)
salt, pepper
2 apples
10–12 prunes
1 onion
about 500ml (1pt) thin chicken or
  vegetable stock
3 × 15ml tbsp (3tbsp) finely chopped
  parsley
3–4 × 15ml tbsp (3–4tbsp) soured
  cream
Almond Croquettes (see recipe)

1 If necessary, cover duck loosely and defrost slowly in the refrigerator for 1½–2 days. Wipe inside with a damp cloth and dry the outside with a dry cloth. The skin should be completely dry, or it will not crisp up during roasting. Season inside of duck with salt, pepper and 1 × 15 ml tbsp (1tbsp) finely chopped parsley.
2 Peel, core and quarter apples. Stuff duck with apple quarters and soaked, stoned prunes. Close opening with skewers. Rub skin with salt and place duck on a grid placed in a roasting tin, back uppermost. Roast duck for about 30 min. Peel and quarter onion. Place onion and duck giblets in roasting tin and pour in stock or vegetable water. Roast duck for 20–30 min more, then turn over so that the breast is uppermost. Turn down heat to 180°C, 350°F, Gas 4 and roast for further 45–50 min. Pour meat juices from roasting tin into a saucepan.
3 Turn oven up to 250°C, 475°F, Gas 9. Baste duck with a couple of tablespoons of cold water and sprinkle with chopped parsley. Leave duck in oven with door slightly ajar until skin is brown and crisp. Turn off heat and leave duck in oven for 5–10 min with door open before carving.
4 Skim meat juices to remove any fat. The transparent fat floats on the

surface and the brown liquid at the bottom is the gravy you need for the sauce. Bring the gravy to the boil and thicken with a little flour worked to a paste with cold water. Boil sauce for a few minutes, add soured cream and season with salt and pepper. Serve duck whole, to be carved at the table, or sliced with butter-steamed, green peas and new potatoes or with Almond Croquettes. To carve duck, see explanation at far right.

Almond Croquettes
(serves 4)
Preparation time: about 20 min
Cooking time: about 30 min in all
Unsuitable for the freezer

¾–1 kg (1½–2¼ lb) potatoes
50–75g (2–3oz) butter
salt
2 egg yolks
a little cream (optional)

50g (2oz) almonds
1 egg white
oil or lard

1 Peel potatoes and cut into pieces if necessary. Boil in unsalted water, pour off water and steam dry.
2 Press the warm potatoes through a sieve or mash with a masher. Beat in butter, egg yolks and a few drops of cream, if liked – the potatoes should have a firm consistency. Season with salt and cool.
3 Blanch and flake almonds. Shape potato into small balls, coat with whisked egg whites and roll in almond flakes. Allow to dry.
4 Heat oil or lard in a deep fryer to a temperature of about 180°C, 350°F. Add a few croquettes at a time, making sure they are not touching. Turn often with a slotted spoon until golden brown then remove and drain on absorbent paper.
Serve croquettes warm.

Roast Duck with Herbs – shown here with Almond Croquettes – makes a delicious dinner party dish.

To carve Roast Duck and Goose
Using a sharp knife, cut longitudinally along breast bone. Loosen breast meat by running the knife closely to the rib cage and cutting meat from body close to the back bone. Cut breast meat into neat pieces across the grain and place back on body.
Press the knife point into the joint between thigh and body and cut off thigh.
Cut thigh in half at the joint and replace in position on body.

Stuffed Duck

(serves 4–6)
Defrosting time: 1½–2 days
Preparation time: about 30 min
Cooking time: about 2 hr
Oven temperature: 200°C, 400°F,
Gas 6
Suitable for the freezer, but will lose
some of its flavour

1 oven-ready duck 2–2½kg (4½–5lb)
salt, black pepper
100–150g (4–5oz) calf or chicken
  liver
20g (¾oz) butter
75–100g (3–4oz) boiled rice
3 apples
marjoram
750ml (1½pt) stock

4 oranges
½ small red cabbage
3–4 finely chopped onions
250g (9oz) long-grain rice

1 If frozen, defrost duck slowly in
refrigerator.
2 Dry liver and duck giblets (optional) and fry lightly in a knob of
butter. Chop coarsely and add 1
peeled, cored, diced apple, boiled
rice, salt, pepper and a little fresh or
dried marjoram.
3 Dry duck well and season inside
with salt and pepper. Stuff duck
with liver stuffing and close opening
with skewers.
4 Place duck breast uppermost on a
grid placed in a roasting tin. Roast

for about 30 min, add 150–200ml
(5–7fl oz) boiling water and 250ml
(9fl oz) stock. Turn duck and roast
for 30 min. Turn again, sprinkle
breast with salt and roast for further
60 min.
5 Chop cabbage finely. Cut oranges
in half using a zig-zag motion over a
bowl. Remove orange flesh. Mix
orange flesh, small apple wedges and
juice from orange with cabbage and
leave in a cool place. Remove pith
from orange skins, plunge into pan
of boiling water and turn off heat.
6 Sauté onion in 15g (½oz) butter,
mix in 250g (9oz) rice and cook until
white and opaque. Add 500ml (1pt)
warm stock. Cover rice and simmer
over low heat for 12 min, turn off

heat and leave rice, covered, until you are ready to serve it.

7 Pour off juices from roast duck into a warm gravy boat, skim off any fat. Cut duck in half lengthways and place on a warmed serving dish. Carving is then done at the table. Pile rice into warmed orange peel halves and arrange around duck. Serve with remaining gravy, rice and cabbage salad.

Roast Duck for the Cold Table

Defrosting time: about $1\frac{1}{2}$ days
Preparation time: about 20 min
Cooking time: about $1\frac{1}{2}$ hr
Oven temperature (bottom shelf):
200°C, 400°F, Gas 6
Suitable for the freezer, but will lose a little of its flavour

1 duck 1.7–1.9kg (3¾–4½lb)
salt, pepper
1 lemon
2 button onions
1 head of celery

1 If frozen, defrost duck slowly in refrigerator. Dry well and rub inside with a halved lemon, salt and pepper. Stuff duck with a mixture of coarsely chopped onions and 2 stalks of sliced celery. Close opening.
2 Dry duck skin with absorbent paper and put on a grid placed in a roasting tin. Sprinkle with salt, pepper and a little grated lemon zest and roast at the temperature given. Turn duck a couple of times during cooking, but leave it breast uppermost on the last turn and leave it for the last $\frac{1}{2}$ hr of cooking. Add a little liquid once or twice during cooking, to prevent the fat sticking to the tin.
3 Dish up the duck, cover loosely and leave it to rest for about 20 min before carving.
Serve barely warm with a salad consisting of crisp lettuce, tomatoes and remaining celery tossed in a vinaigrette dressing and French bread.

Pot Roast Duck

(serves 4)
Defrosting time: $1\frac{1}{2}$–2 days
Preparation time: about 20 min
Cooking time: about 2 hr
Suitable for the freezer, but will lose a little of its flavour

1 oven-ready duck 2–2½kg (4½–5lb)
2 thick rashers of bacon
salt, pepper

2 lemons
25g (1oz) butter
1 × 5ml tsp (1tsp) dried basil
1 × 5ml tsp (1tsp) dried mint
about 300ml (½pt) dry white wine
watercress

1 If frozen, defrost duck slowly in refrigerator. Wipe well with a damp cloth and rub inside and outside with a halved lemon and salt and pepper.
2 Cut bacon into strips and fry in a deep pan until golden. Remove about half the bacon. Add butter to casserole and place duck in it. Turning duck with 2 wooden spoons to avoid piercing the skin, brown on all sides.

3 Turn down heat, place duck back uppermost and add juice from the halved lemon, dried herbs and white wine. Simmer, covered for a scant 2 hr, then turn bird over.
4 Remove duck and place on a serving dish. If you want the skin to be crisp, put it in an ovenproof dish and place under a preheated grill or in a very hot oven for a few minutes, but leave the oven door ajar to prevent burning.
5 Skim meat juices to remove fat, dilute with a little wine or stock and season with salt and pepper. Sprinkle the fried bacon cubes over duck and garnish with lemon wedges and watercress. Serve with gravy and potatoes.

French Duck Pâté

(serves 6 as a main course or 12 as a starter)
Preparation time: 45–60 min
Marinating time: 2–3 hr or more
Cooking time: about 1½ hr
Oven temperature (bottom shelf) 200°C, 400°F, Gas 6
Suitable for the freezer without aspic

1 duck with giblets weighing about 2kg (4½lb)
For the marinade:
100ml (4fl oz) dry Vermouth
100ml (4fl oz) medium dry Madeira
4 × 15ml tbsp (4tbsp) orange juice
2 finely chopped onions
2 crushed bay leaves
½ × 5ml tsp (½tsp) pepper
1 × 5ml tsp (1tsp) grated orange zest
2 × 5ml tsp (2tsp) finely chopped

parsley
For the stuffing:
250g (9oz) minced pork
250g (9oz) minced veal
2 small, grated onions
2 eggs
salt, pepper
stock or cream
200g (7oz) thinly sliced pork fat
For the aspic:
10g (½oz) gelatine
100ml (4fl oz) stock
100ml (4fl oz) Madeira

1 Cut off both drumsticks and pull the skin off the duck. Then cut all meat off bones. Make an incision along the breast bone and separate breast and body meat. Cut meat, liver and heart into small pieces (see picture 2).
2 Place chopped meat and giblets in

a bowl. Mix all ingredients for the marinade, pour over and leave in a cool place.
3 Mix together all stuffing ingredients, add marinade and a little stock (if liked) or cream (picture 3).
4 Cut fat into strips and place along the base and up the sides of a terrine or deep ovenproof dish. Arrange stuffing and duck meat in layers in the dish and fold fat strips over pâté (see pictures 4 and 5).
5 Cover dish with lid or foil with a couple of holes in it and cook in the oven at the temperature indicated. During cooling weight down lightly. When cool, turn out.
6 Soak gelatine in cold stock then dissolve and add Madeira. Pour half-set aspic over pâté (see picture 6). Serve pâté cold, with hot French bread and a green garnish.

French Duck Pâté

1 Assemble all the ingredients needed for the dish.

2 Use a sharp, pointed knife and cut away meat as close as possible to the bones of the duck.

3 Place meat and giblets in marinade and leave for 2–3 hr at least or overnight.

4 Place half the stuffing in a dish, followed by the duck meat and finally the remaining stuffing.

5 Fold fat over pâté and cover with a lid or with foil pierced with a couple of holes.

6 Turn out cold pâté on to foil. Spoon over the half-set aspic to cover top and edges. Chill until aspic is set.

Goose for Guests

Roast Goose with Apples and Prunes (left)
(serves 6–8)
Preparation time: about 30 min
Cooking time: about 3 hr
Oven temperature (bottom shelf):
200°C, 400°F, Gas 6
Suitable for the freezer, but will lose some of its flavour

1 oven-ready goose weighing 3½–4kg
  (8–9lb)
salt, pepper
5–6 apples
18–20 prunes
about 100ml (4fl oz) stock
about 100ml (4fl oz) soured cream

Prepare, stuff and roast goose in exactly the same way as for the duck on page 56, but allow about 1 hr longer roasting time and do not add green herbs. Place 3–4 whole apples in the tin with the goose for the last 15–20 min cooking time. Slice apples and cover with redcurrant jelly to serve. In addition, serve hot red cabbage, gravy and Caramelised Potatoes (see below).

Caramelized Potatoes
(serves 6–8)
Preparation time: about 30 min in all
Unsuitable for the freezer

1½kg (3¼lb) even-sized, firm
  potatoes
3–4 × 15ml tbsp (3–4tbsp) sugar
50g (2oz) butter
salt

1 Boil potatoes in their jackets. Rinse in cold water then peel off skins. Transfer potatoes to a colander then pour cold water over them. Allow to cool completely.
2 Melt sugar, without stirring, in a large frying pan. Add butter when sugar is lightly golden, add butter, stir rapidly and add potatoes.
3 Shake frying pan and turn potatoes until lightly golden brown and shiny all over.
Sprinkle with a little salt then transfer potatoes to warmed serving dish.

1 The goose plus the prunes and apples needed for the stuffing.

2 Brown the cold, boiled potatoes in caramel just before serving.

Marinated Breast of Goose

(serves 4)
Preparation time: 20 min
Marinating time: 2–4 hr
Cooking time: 1–1½ hr
Oven temperature (middle shelf):
200°C, 400°F, Gas 6
Suitable for the freezer, but will lose
a little of its flavour

breast meat of 1 goose
salt
200ml (7fl oz) stock
For the marinade:
1 onion
200ml (7fl oz) port wine
4 black peppercorns
1 stalk celery

1 Cut along the breast bone of the
goose and cut off the breast on both
sides, as close to the body as possible. Place skin side facing uppermost in a bowl with sliced onion,
port, crushed peppercorns and
sliced celery. Cover and leave in a
cold place for 2–4 hr.
2 Drain meat well and place skin
side up on a grid placed in an ovenproof dish. Dry skin with absorbent
paper and sprinkle with salt. Pour
marinade and stock into dish and
roast as indicated. Baste meat from
time to time with meat juices once
the meat has browned.
3 Pour off meat juices. Strain and
skim off excess fat. Turn up the oven
and leave the meat for a few minutes
to crisp skin.
Serve with French bread, gravy and
a green salad containing coarsely
chopped walnuts.

Roast Goose Thighs with Orange

(serves 2–3)
Preparation time: about 15 min
Cooking time: about 1½ hr
Oven temperature (middle shelf):
200°C, 400°F, Gas 6
Suitable for the freezer, but will lose
a little of its flavour

2 whole goose thighs
salt, pepper
1 orange
300–400ml (½–¾pt) stock

1 Dry goose thighs with absorbent
paper and rub with salt and pepper.
Place on a grid in an ovenproof dish.
2 Cut 2 slices from centre of orange.
Squeeze juice from the remainder
and mix with stock and 2 × 5ml tsp
(2tsp) grated orange zest. Pour
liquid into dish and baste meat several times during roasting.
3 Pour off meat juices and brown
skin for a few minutes under a preheated grill or in a hot oven. Skim
meat juices to remove fat.
Serve with gravy, boiled rice with
small slices of soaked figs added and
a salad of finely chopped chicory,
mixed with orange flesh.
Decorate with halved orange slices.

*Below: Roast Goose Thighs with
Orange.*

Index

Almond Croquettes, 57
Apricot Stuffing, 47
Asparagus Soup, 30

Bacon, Chicken with, 42
Baked Chicken Galantine, 18
Barbados Salad, 38
Barbecue Oil Mix, 25
Bean and Chicken Casserole, 9
Boiled Fowl with Cabbage, 31
Boiled Fowl with Horseradish
    Cream, 31
Boiling Fowl, 29

Californian Chicken Casserole, 35
Caramelized Potatoes, 62
Cauliflower Soup, 30
Chestnut-stuffed Turkey, 49
Chicken and Asparagus, 33
  in Aspic, 36
  with Bacon, 42
  Breasts with Chicory, 22
  Casserole, Bean and, 9
  Casserole, Californian, 35
  Casserole, French, 43
  Casserole with Orange, 25
  Casserole with Rice, 42
  Casserole, Spiced, 41
  with Cauliflower, 33
  Cheese-coated Spring, 27
  Coated Cold, 19
  Curried Spicy, 12
  Drumsticks with Vegetables, 9
  Fricassée, 32
  Galantine, Baked, 18
  Ginger, 26
  Greek, 35
  in Green Aspic, 37
  with Green Stuffing, 19
  with Herb Stuffing, 17
  Indian, 34
  Kiev, 21
  à la King, 44
  Liver Pâté, 8
  Mandarin, 7
  Marinated, 8
  with Mushrooms, 33
  Old-fashioned Roast, in Cream
    Sauce, 12
  Olive-stuffed, 16
  with Peaches, 42
  Pieces, Barbecued, 25
  Pieces, Deep-fried, 25
  Pilaff, 8
  Pot Roast, 12

  Ragoût with Giblets, 8
  Roast, 10–11
  Salads, 38–9
  Soup, Basic Recipe, 30
  in Spiced Aspic, 36
  Stuffed, 14
  in White Wine, 26
Coq au Vin Blanc, 44
Croquettes, Almond, 57
Curried Mayonnaise, 37

Deep-fried Chicken Pieces, 25
Duck for the Cold Table, Roast, 59
  with Herbs, Roast, 59
  Pâté, French, 60
  Pot Roast, 59
  Stuffed, 58

French Chicken Casserole, 43
French Duck Pâté, 60
Fricassée, Chicken, 32
Fricassée with Leeks, 32

Ginger Chicken, 26
Goose with Apples and Prunes,
  Roast, 62
  Marinated Breast of, 63
  Thighs with Orange, Roast, 63
Greek Chicken, 35

Indian Chicken, 34

Kebabs, Turkey, 54

Mandarin Chicken, 7
Marinated Breast of Goose, 63
Marinated Chicken, 8
Mayonnaise, Curried, 37
Mayonnaise, Spicy, 37
Mushroom Soup, 30

Normandy Salad, 38

Old-fashioned Chicken Soup with
  Meatballs, 29
Old-fashioned Roasted Chicken in
  Cream Sauce, 12
Olive-stuffed Chicken, 16

Paella, 40
Pâté, Chicken Liver, 8
Peaches, Chicken with, 42
Port-marinated Turkey, 48
Pot Roast Chicken, 12
Pot Roast Duck, 59

Potatoes, Caramelized, 62

Rice Stuffing, 47
Roast Chicken, 10–11
  Chicken Roll, 22
  Duck for the Cold Table, 59
  Duck with Herbs, 56
  Goose with Apples and Prunes,
    62
  Goose Thighs with Orange, 63

Salad Budapest, 39
Salad, Normandy, 38
Salt Turkey and Pea Soup, 51
Sausage and Apple Stuffing, 47
Soup, Asparagus, 30
  Cauliflower, 30
  Chicken, Basic Recipe, 30
  Mushroom, 30
  Turkey, 53
Spanish Pot Roast, 13
Spiced Chicken Casserole, 41
Spicy Mayonnaise, 37
Stuffed Chicken, 14
  Duck, 58
  Turkey, 46
Stuffing, Apricot,
  Rice, 47
  Sausage and Apple, 47
Swiss Turkey, 54

Turkey, Chestnut-stuffed, 49
  Kebabs, 54
  Port-marinated, 48
  Ragoût, 55
  Roll, 52
  Salt, and Pea Soup, 51
  Soup, 53
  Stuffed, 46
  Swiss, 54